Surviving the Suffering

Tim Moore, M.D.

Surviving the Suffering

A Christian Heart Surgeon Looks at Life's Pain

TATE PUBLISHING
AND ENTERPRISES, LLC

Surviving the Suffering

Published by Tate Publishing & Enterprises, LLC
127 E. Trade Center Terrace | Mustang, Oklahoma 73064 USA
1.888.361.9473 | www.tatepublishing.com

Tate Publishing is committed to excellence in the publishing industry. The company reflects the philosophy established by the founders, based on Psalm 68:11,
"The Lord gave the word and great was the company of those who published it."

Cover design by Jan Sunday Quilaquil
Interior design by Ronnel L. Luspoc

Published in the United States of America

ISBN: 978-1-62024-769-3

1. Self-Help / Death, Grief, Bereavement
2. Religion / Christian Life / Death, Grief, Bereavement
12.09.19

Dedication

To Carol, the love of my life and my greatest earthly blessing

Acknowledgments

This work would never have been possible without Ron Plemons, currently pastor at First Baptist Church of Fairborn, Ohio. Ron, quite frankly, is the smartest person I know and is responsible for many of the ideas incorporated herein. It was discussions with him that first led to the concept of different forms of suffering, and it is for his advice, wise counsel, and loyal friendship that I am forever indebted.

My wife, Carol, has been by my side encouraging me and helping me over the several years that this work has been in progress. Without her support, I would never have been able to complete this. Lee Owen has been my personal editor and has given invaluable professional assistance and, most importantly, hope in getting it published. I am also indebted to Lindsey Marcus, my editor at Tate Publishing, whose vision for this book helped craft it in its final form.

The Cardiovascular Surgery Division at Leesburg Regional Medical Center and their tremendous efforts have allowed me to perform heart surgery on a daily basis knowing that my patients are getting world-class care.

Finally, it has been my patients over twenty years of practicing general and cardiothoracic surgery who have demonstrated profound courage as they have undergone suffering. It is from them that I have learned strength and the ability to heroically endure. I am humbled as they submit themselves to my care, praying the Lord's blessing on all of us as we seek to honor Him together.

Contents

Part III : Asking the Physician-in-Chief

Part IV: Other Prescriptions

Introduction

There is no one alive now or who ever lived or who will ever live whom suffering did not, does not, or will not affect. Suffering ranges from the inconvenience of the sniffles to the pain of surgery to the loss of a spouse or the slaughter of millions. It is sometimes real, sometimes imaginary, sometimes earned, and sometimes undeserved, but it is always painful. It is seen as something to be avoided at all costs and to be escaped no matter the price. It leads to fear when it affects us, pity when it affects those we care for, and for some, pleasure when it affects those we do not esteem. In Mark 9:49, Jesus tells us, "For everyone will be seasoned with fire, and every sacrifice will be seasoned with salt." While inevitable, it is rarely anticipated; few plan on when and where and how they will suffer.

When we fail to understand the mechanisms of suffering, we can aggravate the problem. We turn to the wrong sources of relief. We pile high the anguish and guilt. We spend the early morning hours wondering why, and when the answers do not come, we blame ourselves, others, or our God. We wrestle with the uncertainties, and our impatience drives us to find some way to quickly arrest the process. In a society with an attention span of minutes, where problems are quickly solved in twenty-four minutes or less (minus the commercial breaks), we have difficulty grasping that indeed some problems may last a lifetime. Some have incorrectly stated that God will not allow more suffering than you can bear; this is not biblical. What the Bible tells us in 1 Corinthians 10:13 is that God "will not allow you to be *tempted* beyond what you are able." However, you can be faced with more suffering than you can withstand. In 2 Corinthians 1:8, Paul tells how "we were burdened beyond measure, above strength, so that we despaired even of life." As a matter of fact, you can be a Christian and even die.

This book is not designed to minimize suffering. It is not a collection of stories designed to show how another's suffering is so much worse that you should feel embarrassed and inadequate to even be contemplating your own predicament. Thus, there will be no anecdotes comparing the man with no shoes to the man with no feet. There will be little attempt to say, "Cheer up!" and encourage you to simply apply a better attitude to the situation. These changes of a frame of mind are useful in coping but do not address the true intellectual, emotional, and spiritual issues involved.

What this book is meant to do is to provide a framework for understanding suffering and how to approach it in the best manner possible to achieve the best possible outcome. It will not make the suffering go away, it will not remove all of the consequences of sin, and it will not provide miracle cures for terminal illnesses. It is hoped that it will make it more manageable to endure and to prevent one from doing counterproductive things that only intensify the devastating effects of suffering.

As a practicing cardiovascular surgeon, I have seen firsthand much suffering. The profession that I have chosen means that a few people under my care each year will die. I have seen all of the emotions man can feel under these circumstances, from rage to peace, from fear to calm, from sadness to hope. I have seen optimism cruelly crushed and unsalvageable situations miraculously changed. I think that I can truly say that each person's suffering and their response to it is unique. Although there seems to be a finite number of ways that the human body can break down and a limited number of ways that our physical selves can cease to exist, the experience of suffering seems to affect patients and families, as well as their caretakers, in a myriad of ways.

Therefore, there is no single way to correct the problem of suffering. There can be no cookbook-recipe approach to ease the pain of millions of people who, when faced with sufferings common to all of us, bring their own unique constitution, history, personality, and understanding into the arena to square off with their opponent. For some, suffering is a punishment from which to hide, and for others, a chance to demonstrate courage and faith in God.

When faced with treating an illness, as a physician, I must proceed in an orderly fashion to help my patient. The first step is to correctly diagnose the illness. The second step is to determine the *cause* of the illness. The third step is to apply the correct treatment. If you come to me with a heart attack and I take out your gallbladder, then I haven't really helped you very much. Your illness will still persist. And I may make your heart attack worse.

Likewise, *all suffering is not the same*. We must try to identify which variety of suffering afflicts us. Just as the correct cure for an illness requires an accurate diagnosis, we must diagnose our brand of suffering to apply the most appropriate remedy. We must try and avoid complications as well.

Our God, looking down on us, has given us all that we have—our souls, our minds, our bodies, and all this earth and the people in it. Each of these things, during our lifetimes here, is imperfect. These imperfections, which are the ways we differ from the ideal as embodied in Christ, are what yield our uniqueness as well as our sufferings. Given that all is not perfect, our responses to suffering will not be perfect. We will rail against God, we will toss in bed, we will lash out at loved ones, and we will seek someone to blame. This book will not be a perfect solution to suffering with perfect answers. Its author is just as flawed as its reader. Hopefully, despite this, it will lead to a better way of surviving the suffering.

Prologue

> For I consider that the sufferings of this present time are not worthy to be compared with the glory which shall be revealed in us.
>
> Romans 8:18

There are many reasons I didn't want to write this prologue, but I am compelled to do so. This is autobiographical, and it details a part of my life that I really don't want to share with others. It does not present the image of me that I would like others to see; it was a time of weakness, and I always wish to appear strong. There are people who I know that will read this, and they will look at me differently because of it.

People who do not know me well know me as a man of few words. Years ago, when a fellow physician ran into my fiancée one day, he asked her if it was true that we were now engaged to be married. When she told him yes, he asked her, "Well, has he spoken to you yet?"

I would just rather not talk about this.

When I was an infant, I was born five weeks prematurely. This was nearly fifty years ago, and medical care was not as it is today. Because of respiratory distress, I did not breathe on my own for some time. I required a tracheostomy for some time, where they cut a hole in the front of your neck and insert a breathing tube.

I grew up sickly. I was hospitalized many times a year with lung problems. I had two people who I will forever remember as being completely dedicated to my well-being: my mother and my pediatrician. Even with all their efforts, I would often spend half a year in the hospital or intensive care unit. My childhood was marked by much pain. I had intravenous lines and injections beyond count. At age eleven, I had surgery to remove part of my right lung, which was chronically infected.

So I can look back on my childhood and its pain and isolation and wonder, why would God allow a child to suffer so? And as a child, at that time, I would ask, why would God allow me to suffer so?

Many years later, I understand. And after reading this book, you will too.

Part I

The Diagnosis and Treatment of the Sufferings

Sin Happens

> Cursed is the ground for your sake;
> In toil you shall eat of it
> All the days of your life.
> Both thorns and thistles it shall bring forth for you,
> And you shall eat the herb of the field.
> In the sweat of your face you shall eat bread
> Till you return to the ground,
> For out of it you were taken;
> For dust you are, and to dust you shall return.
>
> Genesis 3:17-19

Prior to the fall, when Eve and then Adam partook of the fruit of the forbidden tree, all was well in the world. But with that original sin, man was separated from His creator. And with that fall, suffering began. Things would never be the same again. It would not be until 1974, thousands of years later, that Dr. Henry Heimlich would invent the abdominal thrust maneuver to dislodge food from someone's throat, but I wonder if Adam had performed a holy Heimlich maneuver on Eve before she swallowed that fruit if things would have turned out differently.

We will begin our study by looking at the different categories of suffering, much like trying to diagnose an illness. In our first efforts to understand our difficulties, we must realize that a certain amount of suffering occurs because of the original sin. It does not come as a result of our own personal sin against God, nor does it come with a lesson or as a punishment. It comes from no longer living in perfect bodies while dwelling in an imperfect world. When I get out of bed at night and stub my toe against the chair, I do not see it as a divine message from God. It is because I do not possess perfect vision in the dark, and I lack a perfect sense of recall as to the exact location of each piece of furniture in the bedroom.

Likewise, some human activities are now *supposed* to be associated with suffering. As it says in Genesis, "I will greatly multiply your sorrow and your conception; in pain you shall bring forth children." There isn't much getting around the fact that giving birth, a joy I have yet to experience, is often very painful. And work is now required of us, and for many it is hard labor.

Many of the heart patients I have to treat are born with abnormal heart valves. We have four of these valves in our hearts, each designed like little one-way doors, opening and shutting with each beat of the heart to keep blood going in only one direction. In patients with abnormal heart valves, they do not open and shut easily. The blood swirls around them and flows in eddy and jet currents. In many cases, the blood is ejected from the heart almost in a spray, as if you were to hold your thumb over the end of a garden hose. Sometimes a valve will get stuck partially open, yet not close all the way either, like a door stuck ajar. It neither opens fully, presenting an obstruction to flow, nor does it close fully, allowing blood to leak backward. Eventually these valves may need to be replaced, and heart surgery is required. Although original sin may have decreed that not all people on this earth would be born with perfect heart valves, sin in one's own life is not responsible for being born with one of these valves, and it happens on a regular basis. When a patient is sitting across from me and we are planning surgery for such a valve, I don't usually ask, "And what sin have we committed?"

I am frequently asked if I believe in prayer for illness, and I truly do. In fact, whenever I get a common cold, I pray for healing. And God has never failed to heal me yet, seven to ten days later. What do I mean by that last statement? My attempt at a joke underlies a deeper truth. The seasons come and go. The sun rises and sets. And sometimes we get sick, and then we get well. Sometimes the car breaks down, and we have to get towed. Sometimes the roof leaks. Our bodies and our cars and our roofs break down. We don't always see God's purposes in our suffering. It could be that you got a cold just so you could give it to someone else, and there may be a reason that God wants them to suffer that will be revealed to them. Or the breakdown in your car keeps you from getting involved in a four-car pileup down the road. Or perhaps the person that works on your roof sees you reading your Bible and begins to feel the tug of the Spirit.

The second law of thermodynamics describes how heat always flows from a warmer object to a cooler one. This represents a diffusion of energy, and the process occurs until an equilibrium is reached, at which point no more heat will flow. The process never runs naturally in the opposite direction. The German physicist von Clausius stated this in 1865, and the notion of *entropy* was developed. This comes from the Greek word *entropia,* which means "a turning toward." Basically, in a closed system, entropy tends, or turns, toward a maximum, as things reach an equilibrium. As long as there is a difference between the warm object and a cooler one, this flow of heat or energy can be used to do work. Once the system has reached an equilibrium, it has "run down," so to speak, and no more work can be done. Although entropy has a strict definition in thermodynamics and can be mathematically quantified, in common usage it has come to mean many other things, generally diffusion and disorder, a tendency to "run down" until that equilibrium is reached.

Our universe is one such system. The earth is slowing its turn of rotation. The galaxies are drifting farther apart, and as the universe continues to expand, it is cooling. Scientists predict that billions of years into the future, once the process is completed and equilibrium is reached, the universe will simply be "dead," a cold and lifeless entity. The stars will have burned out, having exhausted all of their fuel, and no heat or energy will flow anywhere. Entropy will have reached a maximum.

This concept of entropy has been stretched to cover all manner of things, including probability theory, information theory, and chaos theory. When we shuffle a new deck of cards, the perfectly ordered sequence of numbers and suits becomes progressively more random rather than more ordered. Fresh water from a river enters the salty ocean and becomes more diffused. As information gets transmitted over and over, errors creep in and are reproduced.

Our human bodies are composed of billions of cells that grow, divide, and repair themselves. After I have opened someone's chest, divided their breastbone, and cut their heart open to repair it, the tissues heal back together, repairing themselves and constructing new microscopic bridges and vessels. Within days, the skin edges are sealed and will not fall open. Within a week, the incision is generally solid. In six weeks, even the divided breastbone is healed. And internally, the heart functions as before, pumping blood with a blood pressure at times as high as two hundred without bursting.

Yet each of these cells must do something that does not seem intuitive at first. They must manage information. The basic molecules of life, DNA and RNA, are designed to transmit and copy information. One form of RNA is even called "messenger RNA." These long strings of amino acids form a code, determining the function of each cell and what proteins or enzymes it will produce. And just like the childhood game of "Gossip," in which one child whispers a message to the next, who whispers it to another, until many children later the message has completely changed, each time the information is copied or transmitted, there is an opportunity for error. These errors are called *mutations.* In addition to naturally occurring mutations, there are mutations caused by outside sources, such as radiation. Damage to the code can come from exposure to the sun, or carcinogens. And when these injuries to the information system occur, they can be copied and reproduced, leading to more defective cells. It is thought that many cancers arise in this fashion.

One of the chief functions of a cell is to repair damage. And when the repair system is itself damaged, things don't get fixed well, or at all. It would be like trying to fix a faltering engine on a car with bent screwdrivers, rusty wrenches, and pliers with one side broken off. Over time, our cells develop errors in the codes, faulty repair systems, and broken-down bodies. We age, and we die.

So I wonder, did entropy exist before the sin of Adam and Eve? Did the laws of thermodynamics change with one bite of the fruit? Did a warm cup of coffee stay warm? I assume they could stay in the sun all day without worry of developing skin cancer. Their skin would remain wrinkle-free, despite the passage of time, and there would be no need for plastic surgeons (or heart surgeons, for that matter). And after a thousand years, their brains would be just as sharp, without senility, and their joints as smooth as ever, without arthritis, and their hearts would beat as strongly as before.

Unfortunately, that is not true for us. Just as our mechanical devices wear out, rust, and break down, so do we. The longest-lived person in modern times has been 122 years old, and on the great bell curve of life-expectancy distribution, we can now expect to live to an average age of seventy-eight. Through science and medicine, we have increased to this point from an average life expectancy of forty-nine years in the year 1900. Yet we do deteriorate, age, develop senility, cancer, arthritis, and feebleness. This is because of an imperfect world, caused by original sin, which exerts its effects from thousands of years ago. Why do we suffer? We may as well ask why do we grow old and die—it is all part of the same package.

And what of natural phenomena originating outside of our bodies? Many illnesses are the result of our interaction with our environment. We are plagued by the inconvenient common cold, the result of a virus taking up residence in our nasopharyngeal passages. Yet many horrendous illnesses around the world are caused by bacterial, viral, and parasitic infections, costing millions of lives. And I am at a loss for why Noah felt it necessary to include two mosquitoes on the ark. Just as Adam and Eve lived at peace with the creatures in the garden, and we will one day see the wolf (not lion) lay down with the lamb (Isaiah 11:6 and 65:25), I presume that in the garden of Eden man and microbe coexisted peacefully, and in the heavenly realm I don't know what the flesh-eating bacteria will do. For now, we must endure these plagues and use whatever wisdom God has bestowed upon us to combat them.

Likewise for natural disasters. Billions of years in the future, when entropy has come to fruition and the sun no longer generates heat, there will be no thermal energy to create the winds and the rains that create tornadoes and hurricanes. There will be no internal geothermal energy to create earthquakes and volcanoes and tidal waves. Christ will have come long before then, but until then, we must deal with these catastrophes as they arise.

This does not mean that God does not have His purposes in allowing these things to happen to individuals or nations or peoples. The illness that afflicts a person may truly serve to accomplish God's will in that person's life, and there is truly a precedent for God visiting natural disasters on civilizations as a means of correction or punishment. In each of these trials, you may study the other forms of suffering and their mechanisms to determine what that purpose must be. However, sometimes catching the flu is simply catching the flu that is common to all of us and does not warrant agonizing over our sinful life.

And I wonder, did Adam ever stub his toe on a rock at night in the garden?

Punishment

> "Arise, take your wife and your two daughters who are here, lest you be consumed in the punishment of this city!" Then the Lord rained brimstone and fire on Sodom and Gomorrah, from the Lord out of the heavens.
>
> Genesis 19:15, 24

The Bible is full of individuals, groups, and nations being punished. Some of the punishments described are so horrific and graphic that it is difficult to believe they actually are in the Bible. The punishments are directed at those who have offended God or abused His people.

In the time of Noah, "the Lord saw that the wickedness of man was great in the earth, and every intent of the thoughts of his heart was only to evil continually. And the Lord was sorry that He had made man on the earth and He was grieved in His heart. So the Lord said, 'I will destroy man whom I have created…'" (Genesis 6:5-7). And therefore, the Flood came and the masses drowned. Sodom and Gomorrah were destroyed with fire and brimstone "because the outcry against (them) is great, and their sin is very grave" (Genesis 18:20).

Pharaoh and Egypt suffered the plagues because of the oppression of the Israelites, culminating in the death of the firstborn of all the Egyptians and, subsequently, the drowning in the Red Sea of all the army of Pharaoh (Exodus). Samson pushed apart the pillars supporting the

Philistine temple, crushing all of the people responsible for his torment (Judges). Jezebel was thrown from her window, was trampled by horses, and her flesh was eaten by dogs (2 Kings 9). And finally, Satan himself will be thrown into the great lake of fire and brimstone (Revelation 20:10).

What lesson do all these people learn from all the burning, drowning, crushing, and trampling? Nothing. These are not God's people, and the hallmark of biblical punishment is that *there is nothing redeeming about it.* The people being punished gain nothing from it. They don't learn from it, don't benefit from it, and don't have their characters developed by it. They have angered God, and they get burned and trampled.

I don't care much for those motivational posters with captions such as "Teamwork," "Determination," "Discipline," and so forth. I figure that if your problems are so basic that a simple poster can fix it, you don't really have any significant problems, and if you do have some big problems, a pretty poster is the last thing you need to solve it. I am much more partial to a company called "Despair, Inc.," and its parody products, "Demotivators." Its posters seem to carry a decidedly less rosy and more realistic outlook on our daily struggles, such as, "Failure—When your best just isn't good enough," and "Trouble—Luck can't last a lifetime unless you die young."

One of my favorites is a poster that shows a large boat capsized, with only a part of the bow protruding above the water. The caption is "Mistakes—It could be that the only purpose of your life is to serve as a warning to others." And I think that is probably one of two useful things about punishment from a biblical standpoint. It serves as a warning to others. For example, if you smoke two packs of cigarettes a day and develop lung cancer, when I deliver the news to you that it is inoperable (and 90 percent of cases are when they are diagnosed), then any lesson you may take from this is likely too late. But your family members, friends, and associates may take from this a valuable lesson that can be life changing. The biggest flaw in this logic is that for the most part, people are quite sure that "this couldn't happen to me," or they wouldn't be smoking in the first place.

I believe that punishment, as described here, is reserved for the non-Christian. (And yes, I am sure that there are people that have accepted Christ that continue to smoke cigarettes. I will deal with that later.) There is no redeeming quality to it. God has been offended, and He exacts punishment. Period. He is the final arbiter and judge of what is acceptable, and there is no higher court of appeal. And that leads us to what may be the second useful purpose of punishment, which is that it may be what it takes for some of us to turn to Christ, thereby adding redemption to it. And in that case, we should actually be thankful *for* being punished.

Well, that seems like a dirty trick, doesn't it? Aren't we supposed to be drawn to Christ by the gospel and the Holy Spirit? Isn't the whole concept of being a Christian made attractive by the promise of a *better* life? We feel that we should accept Christ and Christianity of our own free will, as a *matter of preference*, based on an examination of the available options. Choosing Christ because of the pressures of a catastrophe seems more like a choice made under duress, and, generally speaking, contracts or confessions made under duress are nonbinding. Furthermore, if you are in the midst of punishment meted out by God, why would you be drawn *to* Him instead of running away from Him as fast as you can? (As if you could find some place to hide from God.)

The truth of the matter is that it doesn't matter. God will use whatever means at His disposal that are necessary if He has chosen you to be one of His children. It doesn't matter whether you approach Him on your own two feet, on your own two knees, or flat on your back. Your salvation is what is at stake, and that is a far more significant issue than whatever it is that you are suffering. In this case, the ends justify the means. And if we dare to think that God needs to justify to us *anything* He does, consider Paul being struck blind on the road to Damascus. God wanted his attention, and He got it. And the rest of us have benefited from Paul's life. As much as is humanly possible, I want to learn what God wants me to know *before* He has to resort to such drastic measures to get my attention. A person finding himself in midair at thirty thousand feet is not in a position to question whether it was really necessary to have the airplane fall apart to realize the essential nature of the parachute.

I am a licensed pilot and have been flying for over twenty years. Some may view this as a risky activity, and statistically this is so. One approach to reduce this risk is to eliminate as many categories of risk as possible. How can this be possible? An example would be the category of accidents related to alcohol use during flight. Since I never drink before a flight, that category is eliminated for me. Another category is the group of pilots who are not instrument rated who fly into bad weather or instrument conditions. Although it is certainly possible for me to die in a weather-related accident, since I am instrument rated, that category is eliminated for me. Another category would be those pilots who insist on giving the rest of us a bad reputation and who try to show off and impress their friends by flying low and "buzzing" someone's house or some such silliness. Since I never engage in low-level aerobatics or buzzing, I will not die in that kind of accident.

If you are a saved Christian, the category of punishment is eliminated for you. From the moment you accept the gracious gift of salvation, the things that God allows to happen in your life will no longer be punitive or lacking in redemptive qualities. As the Bible states, "all things work together for good to those who love God" (Romans 8:28). There may be difficult lessons to be learned, sinful behaviors to give up, and pain to be endured, but it will be done with the knowledge that you are loved by God and not ignored.

You can call on Jesus Christ as your intercessor before God and seek His blessings. You can pray for healing, guidance, wisdom, and avail yourself of all of the powers God has that you lack. Strength and comfort beyond your own can be accessed. And importantly, you now have a new instruction manual that you can understand, for the Bible and its Scriptures are now unlocked, and their meanings can be studied. The Holy Spirit will now come and guide you to all learning. All of these things become available to God's children.

If there is anything else to be considered in punishment, it is that it is only the tip of the iceberg. Humans have a limitless imagination in creating punishment for each other, whether it be verbal abuse, humiliation, endless varieties of physical torture, mutilation, or death. The human body itself has a phenomenal number of ways to break down and cause pain and disability. Our work and financial environments lead us into suffering ranging from overbearing bosses to overdrawn checking accounts, from endless piles of work to endless piles of bills. Our suffering may seem endless, pointless, and meaningless, and the discomfort physically and mentally may make some long for death and the peace it will provide. You ain't seen nothing yet.

For the unsaved, punishment on this earth that does not lead a person to a saving faith in Christ leads to unimaginable punishment in the hereafter. We often speak of the gift of eternal life given to the believer, but the fact of the matter is that everyone ever born gets eternal life. Everyone lives forever. It's just that if you have not accepted Christ, an eternal life awaits you that will make your sufferings here on earth seem trivial. You will actually *long for* the good old days when you simply had migraines and bankruptcy and an unfaithful spouse. In this new life, you will be eternally separated from God, with no chance of appeal and physical pain that will never be relieved and mental anguish that will never be extinguished. And this will all be accompanied with the knowledge that this could have been avoided had you turned to Christ.

Knowing all this, I can think of only one person in

history who was already a believer in God, who was fully in God's will, who never sinned or offended God, and who had the infinite punishment applied. Because of this, He who did not need redemption made it available to all of us.

Chastisement

> So David said to Nathan, "I have sinned against the Lord." And Nathan said to David, "because by this deed you have given great occasion to the enemies of the Lord to blaspheme, the child also who is born to you shall surely die." And the Lord struck the child that Uriah's wife bore to David, and it became ill. David therefore pleaded with God for the child, and David fasted and lay all night on the ground...Then on the seventh day it came to pass that the child died.
>
> 2 Samuel 12:13-18

Let me make it perfectly clear here that I am not saying that anyone who has lost a child has done so because of their own sin. This story is taken from the Bible to illustrate the extreme suffering we bring upon ourselves when we, as God's children, are out of God's will. There is no location on earth in which it is worse to be than out of the will of God. He will use any methods necessary to correct His believers, even to the point of calling them home.

For some, this is the most frightening and bewildering form of suffering. This is because there are two categories of Christians who come under God's chastening: those who unknowingly violate His will and those who knowingly do so. The former category, in theory, should be a small one. After all, we have the Bible to give us written instructions on God's will. We have the Holy Spirit to give us leading. We have our fellow Christians and the church to give us guidance. There is prayer and communion with our Father Himself to provide direction. Yet there are many Christians who have accepted Christ as their Savior at some point in their lives who do not read the Bible, listen to the Spirit, attend church, or even pray regularly. Both the shallow Christian and the immature Christian may be deficient in doctrine. In addition, Satan and his helpers will regularly give us bad advice.

When a Christian wife leaves her husband (assuming there has been no adultery or abandonment) and believes this is God's will, there has been some serious misunderstanding going on. This is clearly against God's written instructions. And when calamity later ensues, there is confusion as to the cause-and-effect relationship. I have seen Christians blithely ignore the teachings of our Lord, as well as the counsel of other godly people. They have pursued the path they felt was correct. As it says in Proverbs 21:2, "Every way of a man is right in his own eyes." And when chastening rains down upon them, they are not only in anguish, but they do not understand why this is happening. I have been there myself.

The people who knowingly disobey God are mystifying. They may be able to excuse their actions, just as the unbelieving majority does. They step outside of God's will but believe there is justification. Either that, or they believe there will be no consequences. This falls under the category of *risk assessment.* Humans are notoriously poor at assessing risk, always assuming "it couldn't happen to me." We learn these attitudes because we violate the rules and no consequences are forthcoming—*at least not for now.* We see others getting away with things and enjoying themselves in their sin. Or we think of ourselves as special cases, exceptions to the rule.

In the last chapter, I spoke of people who smoke cigarettes, and if it weren't for them, I would be largely out of work. And yet, there are Christians who do this, and they know it is harmful. When the heart attack happens, they realize that they were not immune to the consequences of abusing their body.

Sometimes it isn't a heart attack; it is cancer. More than a few times I have had to enter a patient's room and sit down and tell him that when I opened his chest to take out a lung cancer, it was inoperable. It is easy to look at this statistically; if you smoke cigarettes over your lifetime, there is a 15 percent chance you will develop lung cancer. If you develop lung cancer, there is a 90 percent chance it is inoperable. Yes, this means that of Christians who abuse their bodies with tobacco, 85 percent will not develop lung cancer. We do not always experience the consequences of our sin in this lifetime. Yet, there is sinful behavior that leads to death. In 1 John 5:16, it says, "There is sin leading to death." And in 1 Corinthians 11:30, Paul writes, "For this reason many are weak and sick among you, and many sleep." God has not given Christians a list of sins that will result in death; He alone has the power to decide what judgment will be meted out against a child of His that strays. And for some, that judgment will be to end their time on earth.

The point is that He will do whatever is necessary to correct us, to get us back on the path, to put us back into the center of His will. God is not a capricious, arbitrary Ruler who watches over us, just waiting for the opportunity to catch us deviating from His will so he can push the "smite" button and whack us good. He cares for us, just as any parent would, and knows that discipline is necessary to keep us safe. Proverbs 3:11-12 tells us, "Do not despise the chastening of the Lord, nor detest His correction; for whom the Lord loves He corrects." Having been under God's chastening myself, I can assure you that it behooves one to not stray. I am actually fearful of being disobedient, knowing what consequences may befall me. I am obedient because I love God and wish to please Him, but at the same time I am acutely aware of what awaits me if I am disobedient. As it says in Hebrews 10:31, "It is a fearful thing to fall into the hands of the living God."

The difference between chastening and punishment, as mentioned in the previous chapter, is that there is no redeeming quality to punishment (unless it leads the disobedient person to a saving faith in Christ). That is not true of chastening, which applies to the Christian. This results in a return to God's will, a re-establishment of communion with Him, a restoration of a broken relationship. In Hebrews 12:11, we learn, "...no chastening seems to be joyful for the present, but painful; nevertheless, afterward it yields the peaceable fruit of righteousness to those who have been trained by it." Once repentance and forgiveness have taken place, our place is once more back in God's comforting arms. And even for the believer who has sinned unto death, his final resting place will be in heaven with our Father Who is most merciful.

The Spiritual "Gut Check"

> I am not at ease, nor am I quiet.
> I have no rest, for trouble comes.
>
> Job 3:26

Many of us are old enough to remember the original *Star Trek* series. When it came out on television, there had really been nothing like it before. One of the more interesting episodes in its third season was called "The Changeling." In that story, the crew of the USS *Enterprise* encounters a machine called Nomad that has just destroyed two planets. It has done this because its mission was to destroy *all* imperfect life forms. It was originally created on earth and launched as a space probe to seek out new life; it had a collision with another alien device that was designed to sterilize soil samples. The two badly damaged space machines merged, forming a new and bizarre mission—to seek out and sterilize all imperfect life. The original probe from earth was created by a man called Jackson Roykirk.

When the *Enterprise* meets up with this new hybrid, its memory had been damaged by its collision, and it mistook Captain Kirk for its creator, and Kirk goes along with this delusion. Nomad decided it needed to return to earth, its launch point, and planned to destroy all life not meeting up to its standard of perfection. Captain Kirk saves the day by convincing Nomad to destroy *itself.* He does this by the brilliant use of logic. He first gets Nomad to admit that anything imperfect must be destroyed. Then he gets an agreement that something that makes a mistake is not perfect. Finally, he discloses that he is not Jackson Roykirk and that Nomad has made a mistake in identifying him as its creator. Therefore, he accuses Nomad of:

1. making an error in confusing him with Roykirk,
2. making a second error in not *detecting* its first error, and
3. making a third error in not *correcting* its mistake by destroying itself.

Whereupon the machine basically commits suicide.

We will take a break from looking at our categories of suffering to look at one of the most important steps we have to take to continue our efforts at self-diagnosis. It is a major turning point in trying to determine the cause of our suffering and requires careful thinking, and hopefully by using the tool of logic, I can show you why it is so critical. Logic is a truly fascinating way to look at arguments. Interestingly, the word *logic* comes from the Greek word *logos*, which means "word." The Apostle John used this same word to mean Jesus Himself, in John 1:1, "In the beginning was the Word, and the Word was with God, and the Word was God."

Logic as we know and understand it today was first systematized by Aristotle in the fourth century BC in a collection of six writings known as the *Organon*. There are several categories of logic, and some can be extraordinarily sophisticated, sharing many qualities with mathematics. There are also many mistakes that can be made in making logical arguments. Such mistakes are known as fallacies, and we must sometimes search carefully to find these before accepting an argument.

One form of logic is known as propositional logic. It is familiar to most people because of its "*If... then*" format. There are two statements, the major premise and the minor premise, which join together to form a conclusion. Together these three statements form a *syllogism*. An example would be:

> If it is December 25, then it must be Christmas.
> *It is December 25.*
> Therefore, it must be Christmas.

The first part of the first statement is called the *antecedent*, and the second part of the first statement is called the *consequent*. If you state that one of these parts is true, that is called *affirming*. If you state that one of the parts is false, that is called *denying*. In logic, it is perfectly acceptable to affirm the antecedent, or you can deny the consequent and end up with a perfectly good argument. For example, if it were true that all Buicks were red, then:

> If it is a Buick, then it must be red.

It is a Buick.

Therefore, it must be red.

That works by affirming the antecedent, or saying that the first part of the first statement is true. But you can also deny the consequent:

If it is a Buick, then it must be red.

It is not red.

Therefore, it is not a Buick.

That works too. But two common logical fallacies are the mirror image of these true forms of argument. They are known as *denying the antecedent* and *affirming the consequent.* Affirming the consequent:

If it is a Buick, then it must be red.

It is red.

Therefore, it must be a Buick.

That just doesn't work. Because it could be a red Toyota or a red Ford or a red Mazda.

Denying the antecedent:

If it is a Buick, then it must be red.

It is not a Buick.

It is not red.

That doesn't work either because again it could be some other red car.

What does this have to do with Job and his suffering?

As mentioned before, the purpose of this book is to lead us to try as best we can to determine which category of suffering applies in order to eliminate our part, if any, in causing the suffering, as well as to not engage in counterproductive activities that worsen it. In the book of Job, we see the classical biblical story of suffering. If you are not familiar with the book, by all means read it. It is one of the most heartfelt cries to God ever described. In case you do not know it, I will try and summarize it.

Job was a blameless man who was righteous in God's eyes. He was very wealthy, with many children and possessions. God even boasted of Job's righteousness to Satan, and the devil replied that anyone so blessed would obviously lead a life that honored God. Satan stated that if God would remove Job's blessings, then he would turn away from God. God allowed the test to proceed. First, God allowed Satan to kill all of Job's livestock and his servants, and then he killed his children. And when this did not cause Job to sin and turn away, Satan afflicted him with boils from head to toe. And Job sat in a heap of ashes, scraping his boils with shards of broken pottery. Yet, "In all this Job did not sin nor charge God with wrong" (1:22) and, "In all this Job did not sin with his lips" (2:10).

Then Job's friends show up, Eliphaz, Bildad, and Zophar. They come to comfort him, and what a lousy job they do! For chapter after chapter, they accuse Job of sinning and explain that that is why he is suffering. And in chapter after chapter, Job denies that he has sinned so greatly as to deserve such horrific suffering or that he has any unconfessed sin. Job has done his spiritual "gut check" and determined that he is not guilty. But his friends persist. Similar to Captain Kirk's logical attacks on Nomad, they accuse Job of:

1. Sinning in the first place, or else he wouldn't be suffering
2. Sinning by denying that he sinned, and
3. Sinning by not correcting his sin by repenting.

It is a wonder that Job didn't self-destruct, like Nomad.

This becomes so painful to Job that he eventually declares, "Miserable comforters are you all!" (16:2). And in the midst of all this arguing and pleading his case, Job does slip a little. Although he never gives up his faith in God completely, he does accuse Him of being unjust. In 9:17 and 18, he says God "multiplies my wounds without cause. He will not allow me to catch my breath, but fills me with bitterness." In many verses, he notes the inconsistency of allowing wicked people to do well and prosper. Finally, a new "friend," Elihu, shows up and spouts off a lot of rhetoric and tries to demonstrate wisdom by putting everyone in his place.

So basically from chapters three to thirty-eight, everyone is arguing based on the following premise: if you sin, you will suffer. This is a very biblical view and based on the fact that suffering is a real price to pay for sin; many people in the Bible who sinned did suffer. In fact, you can sin to the point that you will die because of it, for as it says in 1 John 5:16, there is "sin that leads to death." But can you see the logical error that everyone is making here? Job's friends are affirming the consequent:

If you sin, then you will suffer.
You are suffering.
Therefore, you sinned.

They are totally oblivious to the fact that you can suffer *for other reasons than sinning.* And in this case, that is exactly what has happened because this suffering resulted from an arrangement between God and Satan. And look at the error Job makes in denying the antecedent:

If you sin, then you will suffer.
I did not sin.
Therefore, I will not suffer.

And because he is suffering, he assumes God *screwed up* and is being unjust.

You must understand this. Completely.

Good people will prosper.
Bad people will suffer.
Good people will suffer.
Bad people will prosper.

Your job is not to sort all this out or determine why God allows this. Your job is to do a spiritual "gut check" and determine what your role in your suffering is. What is the cause?

Is this a form of suffering common to all?

Are you a believing Christian?

Are you in God's will?

Over twenty years ago, when I was an intern in general surgery, I was assigned a patient who spoke no English. She was an elderly woman with three sons who adored her and attended to her every need. She was clearly a dominant matriarch in her family, and in her old age, she had become blind and needed a great deal of attention. She had also developed diabetes and vascular disease, and this led to poor circulation in her left leg. She then developed an infection in her foot and was admitted with gangrene.

Each day we visited her, and each day it was clear that she would need an amputation. There was simply no way to restore circulation to her leg, and antibiotics were not enough to eradicate the infection. However, according to her sons, she would not permit it. Each day I would speak to one of her sons, and they would translate to her my message. And each day, she would refuse the life-saving surgery.

One day, after I had thoroughly impressed upon my patient and her sons that she would die without the surgery, her oldest son interpreted for us and told me that she would agree to the amputation. I went and retrieved a surgical consent form, and I sat down with her and her son and explained each and every detail about the surgery. Her son listened carefully to every point I made and explained them one by one to his mother. Once she understood everything, she gave her consent. As she was blind, her son signed the permission form. Her surgery was scheduled for the next morning.

With the help of my chief resident, I performed the amputation, which was actually rather simple. She tolerated the procedure well, and I escorted her to the recovery room. I left her in stable condition. I spoke with her sons and assured them that all was well.

An hour later I received a stat page from the recovery room nurse. My patient had awakened and was screaming hysterically. No one spoke her language, but it was clear she was agitated to the point of hurting herself. She was thrashing and yelling at the top of her lungs. We quickly sedated her, and I went briskly to the waiting room to retrieve her oldest son. I explained to him what was going on and dragged him with me to her bedside. I asked him to find out from his mother what was causing her so much distress. He didn't need to ask her. He knew. He hung his head, looked at me, and said, "I just couldn't tell her."

Unsure as to what he meant, I asked him, "What do you mean?"

He explained that he simply hadn't had the heart to tell her that she was going to have an amputation. All the time I had been sitting together with him and her, explaining the details of the surgery, he had not been translating and interpreting for her. She never heard anything that I had said and had no idea that was what was going to happen.

Now imagine that you are this patient. You are blind and cannot see. You do not speak the language of those around you, but you are comfortable that nothing bad is going to happen to you. And then early one morning someone walks into your room and murmurs comforting things to you (although you don't understand them). And then you are moved over to a stretcher, and they are taking you somewhere, probably for another one of those tests. And you feel a burning sensation in your forearm as medicine travels up one of your veins. And you become irresistibly sleepy. And when you awake, one of your legs is gone.

Many times, suffering is like that for us. We don't expect it, and when it comes, we are bewildered. This causes us even more pain, and we do things that intensify and prolong the suffering.

You must understand this: you *will* suffer. It is guaranteed. Jesus told the disciples in John 16:33, "…in the world you will (not *if*) have trouble; but be of good cheer; I have overcome the world." No one who has ever lived, or who will ever live, can avoid it. You may be temporarily comfortable and not expecting it, but it will happen. And when it does, we need some way, some One, who will help us sort it out. Fortunately for us, we have some resources that my poor patient didn't have.

Most importantly, we have God, Christ, and the Holy Spirit. We can pray for wisdom and guidance and look inward to the Spirit of Christ that lives within us for answers. *And Jesus Christ will never lie to us.* Like the blind woman, we cannot see, and no one will hand us a written piece of paper to explain it to us. Like the same woman who did not understand English, we will not always hear through our ears the truth we need. Yet we can turn to God and ask the necessary "why?" and expect it to be answered truthfully. He may not reveal to you why He allows suffering, but He will help you to understand why this is happening to you, the cause. This will take your fullest attention, and you must not make any assumptions. You must prayerfully seek an answer from God and not try to formulate the answer yourself. It is easy to deceive yourself about the cause of your own suffering (Jeremiah 17:9).

It may be useful to seek counsel from other godly people who might be able to provide insight. This should never take priority over directly seeking the answer from God but may reinforce what you have felt He was providing, or further enlighten. The danger in this is that we may have "friends" like Job, who only condemn us and do not always provide us with the correct answers. Sometimes you need rebuking, to be told of sin in your life that needs correction, and sometimes you need to be made aware of spiritual warfare directed at you. Our brothers and sisters in Christ can be of valuable assistance, but never let them override what God is saying.

And here is the next point. You don't need to spend thirty-five chapters of your life doing this "gut check." You generally need to do this only once. This is really, really important. I can tell you from personal experience that you can spend months or years trying to determine what it is that you have done that has brought this suffering down upon your head, and in most cases, this is a painful waste of time. You need to prayerfully ask these questions and satisfy yourself of the answer. Then you need to *move on.* If you prayerfully go to the Lord and ask Him to reveal sin in your life, He will not lie to you. He will convict you of your sin or let you know that you are not at fault. If God has shown you that you are sinless in this matter, then continuing to tear at yourself trying to figure out what you have done to deserve this is akin to calling God a liar.

I would ask, however, that you remember this. When you are dealing with someone who is grieving, they need love, not logic.

A patient of mine dies, and the family gathers around the grieving spouse who is asking, "Why did this happen?"

And someone will speak up and say, "Bad things happen because of free will. God wanted people to love Him, and to do that they had to have the ability to choose. And when He allowed free will, people had the ability to choose sin. And once sin entered into the world, bad things happened."

And someone else will speak up and say, "Bad things happen to us because they are part of God's master plan, and He works out all things to the good of the believer."

And someone else will speak up and say, "This isn't really a bad thing. They are in a better place, and their suffering is over."

And finally, some wise old person will go up and put his arm around that person and say, "Sometimes we just don't know why God allows these things to happen." And there is more spiritual truth in that statement than in volumes of theological texts.

It's Not Always about You

> God thunders marvelously with His voice;
>
> He does great things which we cannot comprehend.
>
> Job 37:5

In our last chapter, we looked at the story of Job, and we left off at Job 38. This is where God steps in and spells it out for everyone. He demonstrates to all His omnipotence and omniscience. Job recognizes that he was foolish to question God and His ways, and he repents. And then all is restored to Job, plus more. And Job realizes that complete understanding will never be his.

One of the most useful analogies I have heard to describe God's ways is that of the tapestry or rug. Have you ever looked at the underside of one of these? There is a tangle of threads and fibers, with no seemingly obvious picture, yet when you look from the top, you see a nice pattern or picture. And that is what God is doing in our lives, weaving a tapestry. Only we get to see things from below and not the picture that God is seeing. It doesn't make sense to us.

When you read the story of Job, it makes more sense to us than it did to Job. *Job never knew why he suffered.* Job did not write the book of Job; it is thought that perhaps even Moses wrote the book, with divine inspiration. And the part about God and Satan making arrangements for Job to suffer? Why, they were never disclosed to Job. And likewise, we may never know the divine reason that we were appointed to suffer. Many really smart people have wrestled for thousands of years over the problem of why God allows evil. You can do that too, if you have a lot of spare time.

Let us go back to the very first chapter, "Sin Happens." If you have done your spiritual "gut check" and you have determined that you are not being punished or chastened, then you are left with the possibility that sometimes bad things *just happen.* We live in a fallen world, and people get colds and stub their toes and get cancer and are born with bad heart valves. God will work all things to the good of those who love Him (Romans 8:28), but did it occur to you that not everything is all about you?

Job was blameless before God yet suffered. We may all be sinners but not be responsible for the suffering upon us. And to keep persisting in believing this is actually a very self-centered view of things. We are exaggerating our importance in the scheme of things.

In the chapter on chastisement, we began with a discussion of David and his sin of adultery, leading to the death of his son. His sin was clearly related to the loss of his son. And what of the woman who has not sinned who goes to the crib one morning and discovers her lifeless child who has died of sudden infant death syndrome? For her to assume she is responsible for that child's death may be irresponsible.

It's not all about you. Although you are immensely

important to God, He doesn't run His universe around you. You aren't responsible for everything. And to think that you are is inflating your overall importance. Is some sin in your life causing suffering in yourself or others? This is usually not that obscure. If you are committing adultery and your marriage falls apart and your children hate you and you get stuck with huge lawyer bills, your sin is likely responsible. But innocent people are divorced by their spouses, have children rebel, and have to pay lawyers too.

A shuttle box was a tool used in psychology experiments back in the 1960s to study learning, typically with dogs. It is a box with two compartments, divided by a wall lower than the sides of the box so that the dog could see over it and actually jump over it from one compartment into the other. If you gave the dog an electric shock in one compartment, it would eventually learn that it could jump over the barrier into the other compartment and escape the shock. Then, if you sounded a tone or flashed a light before delivering a shock, the dog would learn that was a signal, and eventually simply sounding the tone or flashing the light would cause the dog to jump over. This is similar to what you may have heard with Pavlov's dogs, where ringing a bell was associated with presenting a dog with food, which made it salivate. Over time, the dog would salivate by simply hearing the bell.

But if you take a dog and restrain him in a harness

and deliver the shocks, he cannot escape and learns there is nothing he can do to prevent it. And if you then put that dog, unrestrained, in a shuttle box and apply a shock, he simply lies down and whines and whimpers and does not even try to jump over the barrier. This is a phenomenon known as *learned helplessness.* Lack of control of his environment causes this breakdown.

And likewise, control over our environment and lives is exceedingly important to us, and we will do almost anything to retain it. Conversely, a sense of loss of control over what happens to us can be devastating and may be responsible for a host of mental disorders. For example, the obsessive-compulsive person often engages in rituals designed to prevent awful things from happening. Many otherwise sensible and rational people also engage in superstitious behavior. Michael Jordan always wore his North Carolina basketball shorts under his Chicago Bulls uniform, for good luck. Wade Boggs always ate chicken before every game. And Tom Weiskopf would never tee off without three cents and three tees on him. These are all behaviors designed to control things—in this case, future events over which no one has complete control. It is our desire to be in control of everything that makes us want to be responsible for everything.

And do you remember as a child walking down the sidewalk, and someone would be studiously avoiding the seams in the concrete and saying, "Step on a crack, break your mother's back"? Does anyone really seriously believe that stepping on the joint between two slabs of pavement would result in a spinal fracture in their mother? We would call that a silly superstition, presuming that some innocent thing that we did could cause suffering in someone else's life.

If you eat a bacon double-cheeseburger at ten o'clock at night and wake up at two in the morning with severe heartburn, you would be perfectly correct in saying, "I should have never eaten that cheeseburger!" Your suffering is related to your actions. But if instead you are awakened by a leak in the roof, it would be useless to blame that on eating the cheeseburger. Yet people think like this all the time, and it can lead to great grief and distress. I know several people who currently are in great misery because they are convinced that something they did or did not do has caused suffering in themselves or others. They are in a perpetual spiritual "gut check," some lasting for years. Sometimes suffering happens because of nothing you did or did not do. Sometimes it's about you, but it's not always about you.

Listen Like Sheep

> And when he brings out his own sheep, he goes before them, and the sheep follow him, for they know his voice.
>
> John 10:4

We have seen in previous chapters how in some cases suffering can be ameliorated or unnecessary suffering can be avoided. With punishment, the necessary remedy is a saving faith in Jesus Christ, for by definition this category is for the nonbeliever. It is God's wrath worked out here on earth for those who do not accept His Son Who was sent for exactly that remedy. The suffering is without any redemptive quality, unless it leads the person to accept Christ. The question that must be asked first, then, is, "Is my salvation assured by a saving belief in Christ?"

The next question to be answered, the spiritual "gut check," is, "Am I in God's will?" or, "Where have I sinned?" And we have seen the perils of spending endless time trying to answer that question, as did Job, and how this leads to unnecessary suffering. Sometimes it is not all about us. Sometimes even the faithful suffer. We must prayerfully ask God, Who will never lie to us, whether or not our sin has led to the suffering we are experiencing. Since God does not lie to us, the transmission is not in error. If we have difficulty obtaining an answer, the problem lies with our reception or interpretation of the message.

A story I heard growing up in North Carolina had to do with a troublesome mule. The farmer had tried all the tricks he knew to get the mule to obey him, without success. Despite being somewhat poor, he saved up enough money to hire a fancy mule trainer. One afternoon the expert showed up and looked the mule over. Then he asked the farmer if he had any two-by-fours. The farmer directed him to a cache of lumber behind the barn, and the trainer promptly retrieved a good-sized piece of wood. He walked up to the mule and hauled back and slugged the beast. The mule staggered and dropped to his knees.

The farmer rushed up to the trainer and protested, "What are you trying to do? You could have killed him!"

And the trainer replied, "First thing is, I have to get his attention."

So it is with us sometimes. We have gotten ourselves out of God's will, and He has to get our attention. It works a lot better if we go seeking the answer first, before He has to hit us between the eyes with it. This leads us to the method of the spiritual "gut check." In many cases, it will be obvious. However, we may have to labor to attain this answer. I borrow heavily from the works of Henry Blackaby, in his books, *Experiencing God* and *Hearing God's Voice*, to explain this.[1,2] I would highly recommend both of these books to anyone seeking to know God's will better.

In Old Testament times, God spoke in numerous ways, from direct speech to burning bushes to prophets. In New Testament times, God obviously spoke to us through Christ, through His divinely appointed apostles, and through revelation, among other methods. With a few exceptions, today God speaks to us by the Holy Spirit through His Word, the church and other believers, life circumstances, and prayer.

Of all of these, the most important is God's written Word, the Bible. Whereas what we seem to hear from other believers, life circumstances, and prayer can be subjective and open to interpretation, God's Word is pretty solid ground. Nothing that you ever feel or think you hear should ever be allowed to contradict God's Word. The Bible tells us that we should not commit adultery. Nothing that you think or feel, nothing that anyone advises you, nothing that occurs in your life circumstances, and nothing that you think you might have heard God say to you in prayer makes adultery acceptable. God has laid out to us His revealed will in an explicit fashion in this text.

For those things that are not spelled out in the Bible, God allows us to use the other methods to make a determination. Prayer is essential, for it is our communication to God through His Son Christ that allows the Holy Spirit to speak directly to our hearts, usually in a still, small voice. When presented with information from our life circumstances or fellow believers, prayer should be used to confirm these impressions. Is it a sin to buy that expensive house? God's Word does not address housing purchases. His Word does guide us on being good and faithful managers of our money. We should pray about this specifically. We should look at our life circumstances and whether or not we can afford such a house and manage all of our other financial needs. And we can seek the advice of other fellow Christians (just not ones like Job's friends).

Several important points need to be made here. It is possible to hear another voice speaking to us besides God's. The three likely contenders for our attention are the same ones we have always known about: the world, the flesh, and the devil. All of these—the world and culture in which we live, our own sinful desires, and Satan himself—will try and convince us that what we sinfully wish for is just fine. As it says in Jeremiah 17:9, "The heart is deceitful above all things." We must strive to hear the voice of God and not these other fraudulent sources.

When Secret Service agents are taught to identify counterfeit money, they do not spend time with fake bills. They spend time handling real US money in order to become familiar with how it looks, feels, and smells so they can recognize the false bills when they see them. Likewise, to become familiar with God's voice, we must spend time with the real thing. Jesus taught us in the Gospel of John that He is the shepherd and His sheep know His voice. We must be like those sheep, so familiar with Christ that we recognize it when He speaks to us. The only way to become familiar with our Lord and His voice is to regularly spend time with Him. This means regularly reading His Word and communing with Him in prayer. You can't expect to be able to easily receive and understand what God is saying to you if you only spend time with Him a few times a year.

Secondly, when struggling with conflicting impressions on what to do in circumstances not specifically spelled out in the Bible, we must ask ourselves whether the chosen plan of action will glorify God or ourselves. This simple question can straighten out a lot of confusion.

Thirdly, believe it or not, you may actually want something that God wants for you. There is an old joke about the only diet and heart disease advice that cardiac surgeons give is, "If it tastes good, spit it out." This isn't applicable. This is a spiritual hurdle for many Christians, who assume that all of their desires are fleshly. Essentially, they feel that if they want something, God doesn't want them to have it. This may or may not be true depending on the circumstances.

Fourthly, in my own case, I seem to be somewhat spiritually tone-deaf. I do not always hear God directing me to do something, no matter how hard I try to listen. But I seem to be able to hear, "No!" much better. Maybe it is the result of childhood disciplining, when we often are slow to carry out our parents' instructions but stop cold in our tracks when we hear, "No!" Many times in my later adult life (not my stupid younger life), I have been stopped from doing something that would have caused trouble because I heard God say, "No! You shouldn't do that."

Poor Jonah. He was told directly by God to go to Nineveh to preach the message of salvation. He decided to go to Tarshish instead, in exactly the opposite direction. He was chastened for three days in the belly of a great fish. Only God could have prevented him from suffocation and being digested by caustic stomach acid. Jonah has the distinction of being the only person I know of who did his spiritual "gut check" while actually being *in* a gut.

But there is hope. Just as Jonah repented and was delivered up onto dry land, we also can repent, ask forgiveness, and turn from our sinful path. If we do not, we can expect continued chastening, possibly with fatal consequences. For the Bible tells us (in 1 John 5:16) that there is sin that leads us even unto death. However, God isn't up in heaven just waiting for an excuse to whack us. If sanctification is a journey down a road to becoming like Christ, then chastening is like guard rails on either side to keep us on that road, in God's will.

As mentioned, this book is not about trying to minimize the pain of suffering or simply put a positive spin on suffering. But there is one thing to think of when considering some of Job's questions. Why *do* the wicked prosper (Jeremiah 12:1, Job 9:24, 12:6, Psalms 10:5, 73:3)? Why doesn't God crack down on all these non-Christians who are misbehaving and not living according to His standards? One common answer given is that God only chastens those He loves. Proverbs 3:11-12 says, "My son, do not despise the chastening of the Lord, nor detest His correction; For whom the Lord loves, He corrects." Well, *thanks a lot. That makes everything feel so much better.*

But here is one thing to mull over. Nonbelievers never *need* God. If you sin and don't experience consequences in this lifetime, you don't need God, forgiveness, or salvation. Think about our celebrities and such, people who live their lives with abandon, flaunting their disregard for morals and all that God would regard holy. They rarely experience the consequences of their behavior and never turn from it. Rehab is just a short three-day bump in the road. A rotten marriage is over within just a few months. Adultery is a *norm*. Who needs God when you have a forgiving public, plenty of money, and good lawyers?

The need for God and dependency upon Him are blessings. Those who do not experience these are the ones who are missing out. For all of the great and joyous ways that God can bless us requires that *that* blessing be part of the package. How we wish sometimes that we didn't need God! For we only need Him for those things that we cannot attain ourselves. If only we could provide for all of our own needs, be responsible for fulfilling our own desires, then we wouldn't have to answer to God when we go after sinful things. But it doesn't work that way. God ultimately provides for our needs, and this in turn means that we need Him. And because we cannot ultimately get forgiveness for our sin from forgiving fans, money, and lawyers, we must turn to Him for that need. Pity the ones who don't.

Pruning

> I am the true vine, and My Father is the vine-dresser. Every branch in me that does not bear fruit, He takes away; and every branch that bears fruit, he prunes, that it may bear more fruit.
>
> John 15:1.2

> But may the God of all grace, who called us to His eternal glory by Christ Jesus, after you have suffered a while, perfect, establish, strengthen, and settle you.
>
> 1 Peter 5:10

A young man tries to throw a Molotov cocktail at a house and ends up pouring flaming gasoline on himself. Another young man is a passenger riding in a car with a can of gas between his legs when he decides to smoke a cigarette. An old woman on oxygen at home also decides to smoke. A father of four living in a trailer decides to check for a gas leak outside the trailer and uses a lighter, killing all inside. Another father of three works on a lawnmower and then brings a pan of gasoline into the house and sets it on the stove. On the Fourth of July, a young man sprinkles gunpowder on a barbecue grill to see what will happen, and a very drunken man staggers into a barbecue pit.

Few things can prepare you for the horrors of working

in a burn unit. Even after all these years, the images of these patients are still vivid. The immense suffering and disfigurement leave an indelible memory. For most of us, the only experience we have with a burn is a small burn we inflict on ourselves while cooking, or perhaps a severe sunburn. These people were *cooked.* And what is worse, on top of all their pain, as surgical residents on the burn unit, we had to inflict more pain.

Debridement is a word of French origin, which literally means "to remove the bridle," which likened removal of constricting bands of tissue to removing a bridle. In surgical terminology, it refers to removing dead tissue. For most wounds, this means surgically removing nonliving tissue in order to make room for healthy tissue to grow in. For burns, this is taken to a much higher level, and the burned and dead tissue is excised in large swaths to make way for skin grafts. This means a trip to the operating room, often on many occasions, for the cutting away of the bad tissue to make room for the good. No wonder Jesus used the parable of the vine; the imagery is much more tolerable.

We return now to our study of the categories of suffering with what is commonly known as pruning. Are you everything God wants you to be? Have you completed your sanctification process? If you have done so in this lifetime, you would be the first person to accomplish this feat. The Bible tells us in Philippians 1:6 that we will be finally perfected once Christ returns, and in 1 John 3:2 it says we shall be like Him. Although you may feel pretty good about yourself on some days, I would imagine you fall somewhat short of the standard of Jesus Christ. Even if you have reached your fullest potential as a human being, have you accomplished all that God wants you to? Have you borne all the fruit that He wishes? God prunes us to make us all that we need to be and to produce all the fruit we are intended to bear.

Whereas we may bring chastening on ourselves by our disobedience, we don't ask to be pruned. God determines what in our lives is holding us back, and he removes it. Oftentimes this process is painful, and we suffer during the pruning process. However, it is this necessary trimming that weeds out our undesirable traits and molds us more firmly in the image of Christ.

I haven't yet discovered a way to make heart or lung surgery painless. By using minimally invasive techniques and smaller incisions, the pain can be lessened a great deal. But the price a patient has to pay to have a normally functioning heart valve or to be rid of a malignant lung cancer is temporary pain and disability. This is true of pruning; it requires temporary but necessary pain. If you are a Christian and have not reached your final state of perfection, as I assume most of you haven't, then pruning will be a necessary part of your growth. You probably won't enjoy it at the time.

Jesus promised us two types of pruning. The first has to do with people who are not true believers in Christ. A person who has not accepted Christ as their Savior cannot bear fruit. As mentioned above in John 15:2, those who do not bear fruit are taken away. This actually falls under the category of punishment. And there is nothing redeeming about this. As Jesus further states in verse 6, "If anyone does not abide in me, he is cast out as a branch and is withered; and they gather them and throw them into the fire, and they are burned."

The second type of pruning involves believing Christians, many of whom are doing God's will yet need further refining. As stated in verse 2, "every branch that bears fruit He prunes, that it may bear *more* fruit." This may seem like something of a raw deal because you are a believing Christian, you are bearing fruit, you are in God's will, yet you are subjected to even more chipping away. The price of salvation and eternal life is that you have to be changed from your imperfectness to perfectness, and some of that will occur in this lifetime and the rest in the next.

This process cannot occur outside of Jesus Christ. As He says, "Abide in Me, and I in you. As the branch cannot bear fruit of itself, unless it abides in the vine, neither can you, unless you abide in me" (verse 4). And, "I am the vine, you are the branches. He who abides in Me, and me in him, bears much fruit; for without Me you can do nothing" (verse 5). Just as an azalea cannot prune itself, neither can we. I don't imagine the azalea enjoys it at the time, either.

Well, what exactly is all this fruit God wants? Does he expect me to all of a sudden start producing limes and melons? Christian fruit encompasses a variety of things, and this metaphor alludes to several aspects of the Christian walk. The most obvious reference is to the *fruit of the Spirit*, described by Paul in Galatians 5:22, 23: "But the fruit of the Spirit is love, joy, peace, longsuffering, kindness, goodness, faithfulness, gentleness, self-control." And in Ephesians 5:9: "The fruit of the Spirit is in all goodness, righteousness, and truth." It is commonly noted that this is the *fruit* of the Spirit, not *fruits*. This means that to be described as bearing fruit, you must possess all of these characteristics; in other words, you will not be bearing some fruits and not others. To bear the acceptable fruit, you must possess all of these characteristics. If you are lacking in one of these traits, then you have a fruit shortage, and that sound you are hearing is the hedge clippers being fired up.

The other fruit that is being described is the winning of souls to salvation. Just as seed from a fruit produces a tree that multiplies itself into more fruit, a Christian will multiply himself into more Christians. I am amazed at the fruit some believers produce in this area and how little I do; some are clearly natural "soul winners," but we are all commanded to reach the world for Christ. As Jesus said in Matthew 28, "Go therefore and make disciples of all the nations, baptizing them in the name of the Father and of the Son and of the Holy Spirit, teaching them to observe all things that I have commanded you."

Fruit may also be thought of in the works that we do—not work that we do for living. The good works we do that please God and advance His kingdom are a fruit borne of a branch that abides in Christ. It is literally impossible to be a Christian and not produce at least some fruit or good works. As James says in his letter, chapter 2, verse 26, "For as the body without the spirit is dead, so faith without works is dead also." Again, we are pruned so that we may be more fruitful and produce more and better works.

So as a Christian, we can be saved, in God's will,

bearing fruit, winning souls for Christ, producing God's works, and yet still be pruned in order to make us even better, to grow even more, and to become more of the person God needs us to be. Because God still needs you to fulfill His purposes here on earth, this form of suffering will not be fatal. It just sometimes feels that way.

Nonetheless, this debridement, as painful as it is, is moving forward. There is nothing that I could say that would make it any less painful. I can't imagine that putting a positive "spin" on it would lessen that pain. Listing all the benefits of pruning and how it glorifies God does not reduce the discomfort. But you cannot stop it. It doesn't change the necessity. I have not had anything so painful in my life as dealing with a major burn and its consequences, although I have been pruned. And what is our response to this?

Stand there and take it.

You are probably thinking that I am not in my right mind to say that. But hear me out. If you are in spiritual warfare (which we will discuss later), you are struggling against Satan and the powers of darkness. You must fight back, with God on your side. But if you are being pruned, God is at work, and to fight back against Him is futile and counterproductive. You must let the Surgeon do His work. To quote C. S. Lewis,

> But suppose you are up against a surgeon whose intentions are wholly good. The kinder and more conscientious he is, the more inexorably he will go on cutting. If he yielded to your entreaties, if he stopped before the opera-

> tion was complete, all the pain up to that point would have been useless.
>
> *A Grief Observed*

Struggling against the surgeon only delays what must eventually occur, which is one of the reasons we have anesthesia; we did our work on our burn patients while they were asleep. God must do His work on us while we are awake. How I wish He would do it while we sleep. How I wish I could simply awake in the morning a better man!

In fact, what we are really talking about is debridement of the self. It is that part of ourselves that is holding us back on the road of sanctification that must be excised. But we can't do it ourselves. You can't perform heart surgery on yourself or debride and graft your own burns. God is the one who will perform the surgery. But does that mean that for us it is an entirely passive process? On the contrary, just as we contribute to our own recovery, we contribute to the pruning process. A patient who follows instructions, gets out of bed, walks the halls, works on keeping his lungs clear, and is motivated to get well does far better than the patient who does none of these things. And the prunee who recognizes what God is trying to do in his life, who seeks to cooperate with God in the process by submitting to His will and working with Him will also do far better and will "get well" sooner. Mere words to minimize the pain will not work, but here is where an attitude change can be productive. Refusing to struggle against God and working with Him will shorten the recovery. And less time with pain is generally less pain.

Spiritual Warfare

> ...the whole world is under the sway of the wicked one.
>
> 1 John 5:19

Reinhard Heydrich would make anybody's list of the most-wicked people in history. Born in 1904 to culturally sophisticated parents in Germany, he later joined the Nazi party and rapidly rose through its ranks. His cunning, combined with a complete lack of conscience, allowed him to assume nearly unlimited powers in the Nazi SS and Gestapo. As head of security for these organizations, he was feared throughout Germany, even by fellow officers. After the invasion of Poland, he founded SS "Special Action" groups to effect the complete destruction of Poland, which had a large Jewish population. Jews that were not shot were forced into *ghettos*, where living conditions were so horrible that half a million Jews died there by 1941.

Reichmarshall Hermann Goering then instructed Heydrich to come up with a plan for the final solution, to eliminate nearly eleven million Jews from Europe. In January of 1942, Heydrich convened the Wannsee conference in Berlin to design the plan. The Special Action groups, or *Einsatzgruppen*, began the extermination process, first by shooting. When that was determined to be inefficient, mobile vehicles were designed that could accommodate around twenty people at a time in a rear chamber, into which exhaust gas was pumped. When this method was not able to process enough Jews, they were transported to concentration camps to be gassed with hydrogen cyanide. Six million Jews eventually died in the Holocaust.

Well, by this time, Heydrich was pretty accomplished. He was made Deputy Reich Protector of Bohemia and Moravia (what is now the Czech Republic), and he moved to Prague. His official goal was to increase manufacturing quotas for the German war machine, which he did quite well. While there, he established a Jewish ghetto in Theresienstadt and cracked down on the Czech resistance. His brutality led him to be known as the "Butcher of Prague." He was so good at what he did that Hitler began to consider him as a possible successor in the long term and the director of similar operations in Paris in the short term.

The British felt that they could not allow this to happen. They trained seven Czechs living in England for a mission, Operation Anthropoid, to assassinate Heydrich. These brave men parachuted into the Czech Republic and attempted to kill him on May 27, 1942, first by shooting and, when this was unsuccessful, by tossing a bomb into his car. Fragments of the bomb entered Heydrich, along with upholstery from his car and bits of his uniform, and he died as a result of blood poisoning on June 4, 1942. The Czech assassins were initially sheltered by the Czechs, but then later betrayed; they all were either killed or committed suicide while holing up at a cathedral.

What happened next is difficult to believe. Hitler, in his fury, decided to exact revenge. He ordered the destruction of a Czech village. Lidice, a small town near Prague, was chosen; the reasons for that choice have never been entirely clear. The city was invaded and all the townspeople rounded up. One hundred and eighty-four women were sent to a concentration camp in Ravensbruck. One hundred and five children were taken, of whom eighty-eight were gassed. All 172 men and boys over the age of sixteen were taken to a farm and ten at a time stood up in front of mattresses and shot. The Nazis then razed the city to rubble and burned the remains. What was left was all plowed under and then planted over. Lidice was removed from all German maps. Lidice no longer existed.

Eventually, the Germans lost the war.

Why concentrate on this small group of people in a small village in a small country compared to the huge numbers that died in the Holocaust? Six million Jews died during the genocide. And if you count all of the people that were killed under the Nazi regime, the number may be as high as eleven million.

The people of Lidice were *revenge casualties.* Although millions of innocent people lost their lives during World War II under the evil and cruel plans of the Nazis, these people were executed purely for revenge. Their deaths did nothing to help the Nazis win the war. And likewise, Satan wants to make us revenge casualties.

Satan seems to have had it pretty good for most of history. After the fall, he and his fellow fallen angels, the demons, have been able to have their way with causing misery and havoc upon this world. Even Christ referred to Satan as "the ruler of this world" (John 12:31). But when Christ died upon the cross, Satan was defeated. He *will not win.* He knows this. He is doomed, and his future will ultimately be in hell in endless torment. Christ will not only be coming for us; He will be coming for Satan. Nothing that he can do will change the outcome. Eventually, he loses the war.

But that does not stop him from making his attacks on us. They do not affect the fact that he loses; they don't even delay the time of Christ's second coming ("But of that day and time, no one knows, not even the angels in heaven, nor the Son, but only the Father." Mark 13:32). So as he exacts his spiritual warfare upon us, as horrific as it may be, it is futile. God's ultimate plan for His kingdom will be fulfilled. In the time he has left before being cast into the lake of fire, all Satan can do is try and take out his anger and his fury upon God's children; he can't revenge himself upon God—he can only revenge himself upon us. For nonbelievers, Satan can only hope to have them accompany him in eternal agony.

Therefore, from God's perspective, He wins in the end and gets to determine when that happens.

From Satan's standpoint, he has been sentenced and is out on bail, awaiting punishment. He has a finite amount of time to make everyone miserable, oppose God's work that will be done as He wishes anyway, and then an infinite amount of time to suffer. (And taking this book with him to hell isn't going to help much.) His efforts are ultimately futile.

From our standpoint, God wins in the end, we win in the end, and nothing Satan can do to us changes that. In other words, spiritual warfare does not change God.

It does not change Satan. It does not change our status as saved Christians; it does not rob us of our salvation. However, it can disable us and our work for the Lord. Even worse, Satan can rob others of their salvation as they watch us and how we behave and respond to his attacks.

Since nothing we do affects the final outcome, do we allow ourselves to become revenge casualties? Does that mean that we just go and stand in front of the mattress and get shot?

Hell Is War

> Having disarmed principalities and powers, He made a public spectacle of them, triumphing over them in it.
>
> Colossians 2:15

Once you have determined that you are in spiritual warfare rather than being chastened or pruned (that you are not out of God's will or lacking in an area of Christian development), then it may be that you are under attack in order to defeat you as an agent of the Lord. There are quite a few reasons that our situation is different from those innocent victims of Lidice, and we need not become revenge casualties. There are a few positive things here to consider. To be under spiritual attack means:

1. You belong to God.
2. You are not out of His will.
3. The problem does not lie with you.
4. Your struggle is not with God.
5. You are allowed to and encouraged to fight.
6. God has given us weapons to assist in that fight.
7. Satan is not all-powerful.

8. God is on your side.

Furthermore, God can whip anybody, and God wins in the end.

Having a saving relationship with Jesus Christ means that we are His, and He protects His own; being under spiritual warfare occurs *because* we belong to Him. We do our spiritual gut check and need not agonize endlessly over whether our sin has caused this. As in the category "sin happens," the problem does not arise from anything that we have done, yet there is a spiritual purpose to our suffering. And rather than having God working for us to develop us and move us forward, as He does with pruning, Satan is trying to push us back. Knowing that our struggle is not with God can be relieving. Fighting God is a waste of time; fighting Satan is not. In fact, God wants us to resist Satan's attacks. Defending ourselves against spiritual warfare doesn't change God—He is perfectly capable of defending Himself. Defending ourselves against spiritual warfare doesn't change Satan or his eventual destiny. Defending ourselves against spiritual warfare changes *us*. We are not simply a checker in a game of checkers being used by two opponents, similar to a pawn in chess. We are changed by being in the game itself.

I mean, what are we here for anyway? The Shorter Catechism states that, "Man's chief end is to glorify God and enjoy Him forever." We are here to obey God. We are here to develop ourselves along the road of sanctification to prepare ourselves for the eternal life to come. And part of that preparation is to learn how to fight Satan. That changes us. And as a checker, when we get to the other side of the board, we get *crowned.*

You must be able to discern the difference between pruning and spiritual warfare; a correct diagnosis is crucial. I believe that a key element of spiritual warfare is that the believer is attacked in an area of his strength. If you are walking down the hallway and you overhear two people talking about you, and they mention that you are an arrogant person with a huge ego who demeans the people around them, and you actually are an arrogant person with a huge ego who demeans people, then I wouldn't consider this spiritual warfare. This probably falls into the category of chastisement or pruning. But if you are a kind and gentle soul whose greatest personal asset is humility, you are being accused of these things, and it makes you doubt yourself, your faith, your relationship with Christ, and all that goes with it, then this is probably spiritual warfare. Likewise, if you are a dishonest person and accused of dishonesty, this is not spiritual warfare—this is simply being confronted with your sin. But if you are a scrupulously honest person, and now you are being accused of dishonesty and your reputation is in tatters, leaving you on your knees begging God for His help in protecting you and defending you, then this is probably spiritual warfare. If you are a Christian who is obsessed with money and possessions, God may remove them from you to deal with that lust. On the other hand, if you are engaged in an important work for the Lord that requires extensive funding, Satan may try to cripple you monetarily even though you have been a good steward of your finances. Pruning reveals truths about yourself.

Spiritual warfare causes you to doubt truths about yourself. Pruning is an "attack" by God on those parts of your self that are ungodly. You must not resist. Spiritual warfare is an attack by Satan, and you must use all of your being to resist.

A second distinction is this. Pruning draws us nearer to God. Spiritual warfare seeks to drive us away from God. You may recall a popular book from a few years ago, called *Secrets of the Vine*, by Bruce Wilkinson. It is a fine book, written entirely about that portion of the Gospel of John when Jesus discusses the vine and pruning. He spends a good deal of time emphasizing the importance of distinguishing between chastening and pruning; I think it is just as important to make the distinction between pruning and spiritual warfare because there are very different approaches necessary to deal with these two problems. No one can answer these questions for you. You must again seek guidance by the Holy Spirit through God's Word, your circumstances, fellow believers, and prayer.

Finally, this type of suffering is most likely to occur when you are becoming an effective agent for the Lord. I have seen these attacks occur in people who are reaching out for Christ and seeking Him for the first time, in people who are just beginning to follow Him, and also in established Christians who are beginning a work for Him. Anything that is done that threatens Satan's work is likely to elicit a nasty response. Even deeply devout believers who are doing God's work frequently report attacks by the dark one. Pruning often occurs after a long time of doing nothing for the Lord. Spiritual warfare often occurs when just beginning to work for the Lord. If chastening occurs when we have gotten off the path of God's will, then pruning occurs when we are stuck and not making forward progress. Spiritual warfare, on the other hand, is an attempt by the enemy to drive us back along that road.

How do we fight back? Well, first of all, we don't have the usual weapons that everyone else gets to use. If we are slandered, we don't get to slander back. If we are verbally abused, we cannot retaliate with verbal abuse. And if we are beginning a great work for God and get an attack of gallstones, we can't go give them to someone else. As it says in 2 Corinthians 10:3-7, the weapons of our warfare (the ones *we* get to use) are not of the flesh. The weapons and tools we use are not what you would imagine—no retaliation, counterattacks, or revenge. This does not make sense. With anyone attacking your home or your loved ones or your country, you would use any and all means at your disposal to stop the attack, disable the adversary, and ensure that there is no risk of *another* attack. However, the rules here are a little bit different when your own character is being maligned. And this can make the suffering of spiritual warfare something of an endurance contest; a direct counterattack by yourself, of your own abilities, is not likely to be productive. Satan is far smarter and more powerful than you, having the wisdom of the ages and centuries of experience.

In Ephesians 6, Paul gives us the weaponry that we *can* use for fighting spiritual warfare. I do not wish to dwell at length on this passage. Others have done it much better than I can, and if you listen to sermons for any length of time, this comes up frequently. In brief, Paul is using an analogy of a soldier of Rome and his armor. In Ephesians 6:10-17, we are to put on:

1. The belt of truth, for Satan will attack us with lies and deception,
2. The breastplate of righteousness, for Satan will accuse us before God of being unrighteous, and of our own sinful nature,
3. The shoes of the gospel of peace, for we are endowed with peace from our God in our time of conflict,
4. The shield of faith, for it is by our faith that God provides us with protection from Satan's attacks,
5. The helmet of salvation, by which we are assured of our relationship with God (which Satan will cause us to doubt), and
6. The sword of the Spirit, which is the Word of God, and our only offensive weapon.

Well, that's all fine and good. I did this when I first met spiritual warfare and read the books on how to deal with it. Got up; strapped on the belt, the breastplate, the shoes, the helmet; picked up the shield and sword; and went out to battle the forces of darkness. Got kicked onto my butt.

I want to direct you to something that I think is at

least as important as *any* of the listed armor. Read a little further into verses 18 and 19, and Paul says "praying always with all perseverance and supplication for all the saints—*and for me*, that utterance may be given to me…" Paul is asking *other Christians to pray for him*, and this leads me to what I think is the single most important truth in this book. If you cannot remember anything else I have written, please just tear this page out and cut out the following sentence: *Never fight your spiritual battles alone.*

Forget this "army of one" stuff. Forget Schwarzenegger and Stallone fighting off huge armies of bad guys by themselves. Satan is smarter than you. He is more powerful than you. He has centuries more experience than you. He has a host of demons trained to fight you. You need all the help you can get.

Obviously, you need Jesus Christ. That is why you should have a saving relationship with Him.

But you need more soldiers. You need people praying for you. You need people to whom you can talk with, pray with, take your problems to, receive strength from, learn from, and cry with. You need experienced soldiers who have been there. You need spiritual generals, who know how to marshal other resources for you. You need inexperienced Christians who only know to offer simple prayers for you because they have a heart for God. You need people who can provide spiritual food for you and nurse your spiritual wounds. This can often be a problem for men, who insist on taking care of all their problems themselves. As a man, you must be humble enough to reach out to others and say, "I have this spiritual attack going on, and I need your help." This is why you go to church and meet with other believers. I believe that having other Christians on our side is our most important spiritual weapon.

It may help to realize that this wouldn't be happening in the first place unless you are one of God's chosen people. Satan can try to cripple us and inflict misery upon us as a matter of revenge, but he cannot ultimately thwart God's will. He can also try and take as many people to hell with him as he can. This is the ultimate, eternal revenge casualty. By having a saving relationship with Jesus Christ, you can avoid this. But remember this: people who are not saved will be watching you fight your spiritual battle. How you conduct yourself may determine which side someone else chooses, and this determines his ultimate destiny. For we all are created for eternal life. Some will spend eternity in heaven. Some will spend it in the lake of fire.

There is hope. We do not have to be a revenge casualty. We do not simply have to stand in front of the mattress and get shot. We can fight back. Satan is not God. He was created by God. He is not all knowing. He is not all-powerful. And he is not present everywhere. He must rely upon his associates, the demons, or other fallen angels to do his work. He and his workers can be defeated by a combined force of God, yourself, and a whole bunch of other checkers.

For the Glory of God

> Now as Jesus passed by, He saw a man who was blind from birth. And his disciples asked Him, saying, "Rabbi, who sinned, this man or his parents, that he was born blind?" Jesus answered, "Neither this man nor his parents sinned, but that the works of God should be revealed in Him."
>
> John 9:1-3

> But I say to you who hear: Love your enemies, do good to those who hate you, bless those who curse you, and pray for those who spitefully use you.
>
> Luke 6:27-28

Most Americans alive today cannot remember World War II. There are some that can remember the Korean War, and many can remember Vietnam. But the modern concept of warfare as we know it in the American consciousness is that of the two Gulf wars. Heavily superior American firepower and technology made short work of the opposition, at least in terms of the battlefield. But it was not always this way.

We are used to quick victory and low casualties. To date, we have lost four thousand Americans in the Iraq conflict. But we lost roughly:

800,000 in the Civil War
300,000 in World War I
450,000 in World War II
30,000 in Korea
50,000 in Vietnam

In the early days of World War II, the United States was in serious trouble. We were fighting a war on two fronts, against Germany and Japan. And things weren't going well in the Pacific. In addition to the huge losses at Pearl Harbor, we suffered defeats in the Philippines, Guam, and Wake Island. The Japanese basically owned the Pacific west of Hawaii.

The Japanese appeared unstoppable, and American morale was at a low. President Roosevelt wanted to mount a strike against Japan to somehow show we were not at their mercy. Lieutenant Colonel Jimmy Doolittle was recruited to lead such a mission. This was a bold and daring attempt at doing something no one had attempted before. After innovative training, a group of B-25 twin-engine bombers (not aircraft carrier fighters) and their crews were boarded onto the aircraft carrier USS *Hornet*. A task force sailed for Japan with plans to launch the planes four hundred miles from Japan with targets in Tokyo, Osaka, Yokohama, and Nagoya. After bombing Japan, the planes were to continue on to China, where they would refuel and then continue to safety. But the task force was spotted by a fishing vessel seven hundred miles out, and this required the bombers to depart sooner than expected, in hazardous weather, on April 18, 1942. After a successful mission delivering their bombs on target, they headed for safety. Because they had departed early, they all ran out of gas near the China coast, and only one reached a safe airfield in Russia. The remainder of the planes either crashed on the China coast or the crews bailed out. One member of the raid died while doing the latter.

Of the sixteen bomber crews of five each, two crews ran into serious trouble. The crew of Dean Hallmark lost two members in a crash landing, and the remaining three were captured. All of the members of William Farrow's crew were taken prisoner. The Japanese were furious that their homeland had been successfully attacked, and much wrath was incurred by these fliers. All eight were subjected to starvation and brutal torture. They were beaten. They were subjected to water torture, with water poured down their noses and mouths until they drowned, then were resuscitated. They were made to kneel with thick bamboo poles behind their knees, and their captors would jump up and down on their thighs. They were strapped into machines that were cranked until they thought they would be stretched apart. They were hung by handcuffs placed over pegs. They were placed in straightjackets tightened so they couldn't breathe. They had pencils shoved into their hands between their fingers, then the fingers were clasped together and the pencils rolled around.

A quick trial was held by the Japanese. The fliers were convicted of criminal acts and sentenced to death. On October 15, 1942, three of the airmen, Dean Hallmark, William Farrow, and Harold Spatz, were led to a field, made to kneel, and their arms were raised in a crosslike position. Hoods were placed over their heads, and an ink mark was made over their foreheads. They were executed by firing squad.

The remaining five continued to endure mistreatment. One of these, Bob Meder, assumed the role of encourager. He frequently devised games to keep up morale. He eventually caught dysentery and died on December 1, 1943, and his death had a profound impact on the other four. As 1944 came around, the Japanese were on the defensive and realized that if they lost the war, they would be held accountable for the treatment of these American prisoners. They were granted books, and one of these was the Bible. The prisoners shared the Bible and memorized passages. They were allowed to keep it for three weeks.

By the summer of 1945, all were near death from disease and malnutrition. After the dropping of the atomic bombs on Hiroshima and Nagasaki, the surrender of Japan seemed imminent. Special teams were brought into China to rescue American prisoners as soon as possible because it was feared that the Japanese might execute them as a matter of honor. The four survivors of the Doolittle Raid—Chase Nielsen, Jacob DeShazer, Robert Hite, and George Barr—were rescued and avoided becoming revenge casualties. They were eventually returned to the United States to try and resume something of a normal life.

How does this story make you feel? Angry? Outraged at the mistreatment of soldiers who were performing their duty? And if you were to put yourself in the place of one of those men, how would you feel toward your tormentors? When you returned to the United States and suffered from the chronic results of severe malnutrition and looked at your scars and tried to make your hands work, what would you feel? How would you go on?

When he was in that prison cell, Jacob DeShazer was profoundly affected by the Bible verses he read. To quote *Four Came Home* by Carroll V. Glines,

> His hatred for his captors slowly vanished as he experienced a "revelation" in which he believes that the Lord spoke to him and urged him to show "faith as a grain of mustard seed."[3]

DeShazer said, after nearly getting his foot broken, "Instead of hatred and bitterness toward the guard, I remembered the words of Jesus who said, 'Love your enemies, bless them that curse you, do good to them that hate you, and pray for them which despitefully use you, and persecute you.'"

DeShazer eventually became a missionary to the Japanese. He received a master of divinity degree. He and his wife planted twenty-three churches in Japan. He was instrumental in leading Mitsuo Fuchida to accept Christ; Fuchida was the lead pilot in the attack on Pearl Harbor. He spent his life ministering to and preaching the gospel to the country that had taken the lives of his fellow fliers and had inflicted so much pain upon him. He took his suffering and turned it into glory for God. Reverend DeShazer died in March of 2008 at the age of ninety-five.

I tell you right now, outside of a miracle worked on me by Jesus Christ, I just don't think I could do that. I would consider myself holy before God by not trying to exact revenge against those people who tortured me.

I think I might have enough of Jesus Christ in me to not go and seek retribution. But to love those people and spend my life devoted to them and minister to them? It would take more than godly heart surgery on me, more than patching things up. It would take a heart transplant.

I began a Bible study in January 2001 with Bible Study Fellowship, an international nondenominational Bible study with participation around the world. Our group met in the evenings, and meetings would begin with gathering together as a large group for worship music and prayer. Then the group would break up into small groups to discuss the answers to questions handed out the week before. At the conclusion of the small-group session, members were asked if there were any prayer concerns. Then all the small groups joined together again, and a lecture was given on the Bible material just addressed by the questions from the prior week. As the assembly was dismissed, members picked up a course syllabus that further explained the previous week's material, and new questions and reading assignments were given for the week ahead.

As I joined my small group halfway through the year, I remained somewhat silent, trying to figure out how all this worked. I did not know any of the small group members. And when it came time for our little group's members to share their needs for prayer, I listened as men related the things for which they wanted the group to pray for them. One man needed a job after recently becoming unemployed. Another had a troubled marriage. One gentleman had a child who was having behavioral problems. And then there was Custer (with the archaic name of a general known for dying in a futile battle), who needed help preparing to die.

Well, this made the other prayer needs seem a lot less of a big deal. Custer had had cancer and now had a recurrence and was told it was terminal. A devout Christian, he had made his peace with God and was now asking for prayer as he prepared to leave his loving family behind. I listened each week and was struck by his dignity and his concern for others. In fact, his biggest prayer concern was for his family. As a new member, I did not feel I knew him well enough to ask questions. Eventually, however, curiosity overcame me, and I privately asked our small group leader to give me some insight. He told me that Custer had colon cancer that had spread to his lungs.

I approached Custer one evening and asked him for his story. He had colon cancer, and when it was first discovered, it had already spread to his liver. At the time, he was in his early fifties, and he underwent surgery for a colon resection and to remove the tumor in the liver. He took chemotherapy but developed a recurrence in his liver; this was treated by implanting a pump that delivered chemotherapy directly into his liver. This worked for a while, but eventually he began growing tumors in his lungs. His doctors had told him to begin making final preparations.

I had experience with cancer that had spread to the lungs, and I asked Custer if he would mind if I reviewed his CAT scans. He obliged, and one night after Bible study he handed them over. I sat in my kitchen that night, holding the scans up and counting the tumors and their size. They could be removed surgically.

I asked Custer if he would consider this; it meant two separate operations, one on his right chest and one on his left, and both would be painful and require extensive recovery. It didn't take long before he decided to go for it, and we decided to tackle the left side first, as it was the most difficult side. There was one problem; it was possible that one of the tumors on the left side was in a lymph node as opposed to being in the lung itself, and this had huge implications.

The rules for operating on cancer that has spread to the lungs are as follows: (1) The primary cancer has been removed, (2) There is no other cancer in the body except in the lungs, and, (3) All of the lung tumors can be removed. At this point, Custer met all of these criteria, and if successful, he had a 50 percent chance of surviving. There was one exception to these rules. If the cancer had spread to any of the lymph nodes in the chest, he would die in less than two years. No amount of staring at the scans could tell me if this round nodule was in the lung tissue itself or an adjacent lymph node. There would be no way to determine this until the surgery itself.

In May of 2002, I found my hands inside Custer's left chest. I had exposed the tumors. Two were clearly in the lung tissue and were easily excised, taking only small surrounding portions of the lung tissue. The largest one, the one in question, presented a problem. It was in a location that could prove to be either lung or lymph node, but worse than that, to get it out, I would have to remove half of his left lung. I debated whether or not to put him through such a procedure if he were only to die in the next several months. I was on the verge of closing his chest, which meant sending him home to make those final preparations.

Before making such a decision, I began praying for guidance. Sensing God's leading, I proceeded to remove the tumor and half of the lung. It came out easily, and after surgery, we waited for the pathology results. They showed that the tumor was in the lung and not a lymph node. Encouraged by these results, we removed the right lung tumors six weeks later.

God had moved so clearly in our midst. He had led me to Bible Study Fellowship, He had led me to Custer's group, and He had led me to ask about Custer's illness. He had encouraged Custer to undergo the surgery, and He had guided me during the most difficult part of the operation to do the correct thing. He had blessed Custer with rapid healing and recovery, and seemingly, a cure.

His cancer came back two years later. He developed more tumors in his liver. He had some experimental therapy that didn't work, and he basically lived on chemotherapy for the next few years, despite the disabling side effects. Finally, the cancer obstructed the drainage of bile produced by the liver, and he developed jaundice. He lost weight. The end was near.

In desperation, we found a liver surgeon who felt that removing most of his liver might be possible. It would be another risky procedure, but his only chance. He traveled to a major medical center, and I went up with him the night before and had dinner with him and his wife.

He understood that he might not survive the surgery the next day. His spirits were good the next morning, and he survived the huge operation. He had numerous complications but pulled through. Despite his weakened condition and the extreme effort required, he returned to Bible study. He saw his daughters graduate from school. He inspired those around him. And his cancer still came back. I saw him in the hospital, and when I asked him how he was doing, he said, "Spiritually, I'm on top of the world." He died at home a few weeks later, surrounded by his loving family.

During this time that I knew him, he never complained about his sickness. He did not complain that he had cancer. He did not complain about the pain or side effects of the chemotherapy. He did not complain about the pain of his many operations. He did not complain when his treatments failed. His only concern was for his family and spreading the gospel of Christ Jesus.

What did he do since he didn't spend his time complaining? He glorified God in all that he did. He was faithful in attending his Bible study and was an inspiration to all who saw him. His life was a testimony to God's power. He shared the gospel with anyone who would listen. When questioned about his illness, he would use it as a springboard to talk about the Lord. As he was being prepared for his last operation, the one that might take his life, he witnessed to the nurses getting him ready. He delivered sermons at churches. He praised God to the very end.

What sin did Custer commit to deserve such suffering? What sin did Custer's parents commit to warrant such a thing? None. God chose him for suffering that He might be glorified. What a horrible thing! How awful to be used as nothing more than a tool of an uncaring, manipulative God Who would allow pain and misery on such a faithful servant, just so His reputation might be enhanced? Custer didn't see it that way.

You see, being a real man doesn't mean shooting at the bad guys with a gun in both hands. It doesn't mean being a top secret agent who gets several women into bed in the process of completing his mission. It doesn't mean dancing in the end zone. Being a real man is taking the absolute worst that this world can hand you and using it to glorify God. Custer didn't look at his cancer as a curse; he looked at it as an honor, to be chosen to fulfill God's purposes and His will. He realized that however limited his time on this earth, he would be welcomed into heaven as a good and faithful servant.

We never really know how we would react given the diagnosis of a fatal illness. Could you use this terrible event to glorify God, praising Him? Satan cannot rob us of our salvation. He can rob others of their salvation as they watch a Christian and how they respond to their suffering. Could you use it as an opportunity to lead more people to believe in Him? Would you be able to describe God's work in your life and how your terminal illness was leading you closer to Him without complaint and blame? Would your primary concern be for those left behind and for those who had not yet chosen eternal life with Christ?

Could you be a Custer?

Maybe all glorification of God through suffering requires that He work some kind of miracle in the life of a believer. And ask yourself, would you take a horrible disease upon yourself just so that God could demonstrate His glory by affecting a miraculous cure? More importantly, would you take such an illness upon yourself, *without* a miraculous cure, just so you could glorify God by your actions? It takes a miracle from God for us to be able to glorify Him when there is no other miracle forthcoming.

To do so would require a shift in thinking. First, you must stop asking the question of why God allows suffering. No one has yet come up with an answer to the deaths of those six million Jews in the Holocaust. Assuming you are a saved Christian not enduring punishment, you must determine if you are being chastened or pruned or in spiritual warfare. But if you are suffering, and it's not because of being out of God's will, lack of fruit, or because you are under spiritual attack, then you must not waste endless time doing a spiritual gut check. Now you are stuck with just *suffering*. What are you going to do about it?

In this category, there is nothing that you can do to prevent it, such as accepting Christ to prevent punishment or making certain you are not disobedient, in order to avoid chastening. There is nothing you can do to lessen it, such as giving up or sacrificing something to God's pruning or resisting Satan in fighting a spiritual battle. This is God's sovereign will. Like Job, you don't get the answers. Yet if you cannot do anything, then you can endure. This can be done in a way that glorifies God or not. I have seen endless numbers of patients with severe, intractable illnesses who somehow managed to demonstrate godly behavior in the midst of their suffering. I am in awe of them.

I had a patient many years ago who arrived in the hospital near death from a huge heart attack that caused his heart to rupture. He was in shock, and emergency surgery was necessary. I explained to him that his condition was terrible, and although he might not survive, we needed to rush off to the operating room in an effort to try and save his life. His last words on this earth to his family were, "And make sure my brother doesn't get any of my money!" Whom does that glorify?

What is God's ultimate plan for me, and if I cannot discern it, what can I do now that will bring glory to God? It is this perspective, the forward-looking one, that is the most difficult one to develop. You see, our present is the future's past. We cannot know how what we are going through right now will ultimately be used to glorify God in the future. We may never know. We must pray to God to work that miracle in us that will allow us to do what we cannot do of our own. Just as Jacob DeShazer did in his prison cell over sixty years ago.

For Christ

> If the world hates you, you know that it hated Me before it hated you.
>
> John 15:19

> Yes, the time is coming that whoever kills you will think that he offers God service.
>
> John 16:2

> Yes, and all who desire to live godly in Christ Jesus will suffer persecution.
>
> 1 Timothy 3:12

It is the year AD 126. A youthful girl of seventeen, your parents named you Laelia. Your father and mother accepted Christ before you were born, and this is your deep, dark family secret. You worship with other Christians in hiding, usually no more than three families together at any one time. You yourself took Christ as your Savior when you were eleven. Hadrian is the emperor of your city, Rome.

It was a week ago that the soldiers came for your family and tore you from your home. Your father suspects that it was your uncle who gave your family's name to the authorities. Since then, you have been kept in prison, cold and dark, and with little to eat. And you know what is going to happen. And you know that you have the power to prevent it, if only you will deny Christ.

The stories that have been whispered are vivid in your memory. Foremost is that of Ignatius, the bishop of Antioch. Two years before you were born, he was brought before the emperor Trajan. Fellow Christians were being persecuted for their beliefs, and Ignatius felt that if he submitted to the emperor, the fury would be averted. And so he was taken to Rome and thence to the Coliseum.

Trajan offered him his life, if only he would sacrifice to the gods of the Roman Empire, and Ignatius replied, "I wish to go with Jesus, who is the bread of immortality and the drink of eternal life; I live entirely for Him, and my soul yearns for Him. I despise all your torments, and I cast at your feet your proffered liberty…it is permitted that I come to God, whom I desire with an insatiable desire; I am His corn, and must be ground under the teeth of the beasts to become for Him a pure and white bread."

And while standing in the midst of the Coliseum, lions were released, and as it is written in the *Acts of the Martyrs*, "His prayer was heard, the lions left nothing but the harder bones of his body."

And now, Hadrian has succeeded Trajan and has carried on his persecution with enthusiasm. Although you will never know it, nearly ten thousand Christians will lose their lives during his reign. This morning they transferred you and your family to the hypogeum, the underground portion of the Coliseum. You are tired, hungry, and scared. Little Marius, your brother, is brave. And so are your parents, who have been praying continuously. All the things you had thought of during the last year—taking a husband and having children of your own—seem so far away now. Because you know what is going to happen.

The weather today is spectacular, a cool day with few clouds in the sky. The fall harvest has been bountiful, and as you were led through the streets, it was obvious the city was full. Crowds filled the markets, and the vendors busily sold their wares. Above you, the Coliseum begins to fill. Although it is early, many have been drinking. For the citizens of Rome, this venue is more entertainment than anyone could hope for. There will be hunting of beasts—exotic animals from far-off lands, such as the rhinoceros and ostrich. There will be the execution of criminals. There will be reenactments of famous battles. And, of course, the greatest attraction of all: the contest between gladiators. The Coliseum is a stadium where death is common, and common things fail to excite when seen regularly. Novel excitements must continually be brought before the crowds.

No one knows what to think of the Christians. They are a strange people, keeping to themselves, refusing to worship the Roman gods, and talking of this bizarre religion where their God actually lives inside them. And the Roman emperors have seen them as a significant threat, one that cannot be ignored. What better way to expose them to the public than to incorporate them into today's show? The crowd is already cheering the early entertainments. And you know what is going to happen.

You are so young! And there was so much to look forward to. And today you will die, simply because of the God your family worships. You have hurt no one; you have not stolen or lied or murdered, yet you will not see another sunset. Your death will mean so little. Your death will simply be entertainment, a sport, rapidly forgotten as new and varied acts follow yours. It is difficult to look at young Marius, who clings to your mother. He too knows what is going to happen, yet no tears stain his cheeks.

Who is this Christ who demands your life? You can live, if only you deny Him and agree to worship the Roman gods. It would be so simple to do and then to walk into the sunlight outside of this Coliseum. But your father has repeated the words of this Christ: "Therefore whoever confesses Me before men, I will also confess before my Father who is in heaven. But whoever denies Me before men, him I also deny before my Father who is in heaven." And your father tells you that the life that begins as this one ends is far greater than one can imagine.

The guards have come to your cell, and you hear the large key turn the rusty tumblers to the lock. Bound together in chains, you walk up the stairs slowly. Near the top, the sun breaks through the opening, temporarily blinding you after being in the dark for so long. There are two other families with you, also with children. As you step onto the bloody sand of the Coliseum, the crowd roars in anticipation of the next act. Quietly, without uttering a word, you are led to the center of the amphitheater. Your father, so calmly, requests that everyone kneel to pray. Everyone joins hands. It is hard to concentrate because you know what is going to happen.

The crowd is amused at these Christians and their silly, impotent God who is certainly unable to save them now. And it is difficult to decide what to pray; divine deliverance does not seem possible. And so you pray for quick and merciful death for you and your family and that God will be glorified in all that happens. A roar goes up from the crowd as the lions are released. They are hungry, having not been fed for five days. And their handlers harass them, provoking them to savage anger. As they approach, you can smell them. Prayers are lifted up from your circle of family and friends, and your mother's tears begin to flow as your father looks toward the sky. Marius holds tight to his mother, and you reach for your father. The beasts are upon you, and now you can smell not only their odor but their hot and foul breath. The lion closest to you stops for just a second and then pounces, throwing you on your back. His jaws clamp down on your shoulder, and the pain is excruciating as he shakes his head. As the light becomes dimmer in your eyes, you can hear the agony escape the lips of Marius and your parents, even as the crowd roars. You have become spectacles. You have become martyrs.

I have absolutely no authority to write this chapter. While I have experienced most of the different types of suffering in this book, I have never been called upon to suffer for Christ. I suspect that in this day and time, hardly anyone in this country has truly suffered for Christ. A Christian may be exposed to rude language, have his senses assaulted by the immoral society around him, or, at worst, be the butt of someone's joke. He may be offended by the atheistic movement that has picked up steam in recent years, but none of these qualifies as suffering for our Lord and Savior. Yet people around the world have been persecuted, even unto death, simply because they professed Jesus as their God, above all others.

Persecution of Christians continues today. In India, missionaries have been murdered, churches ransacked, and nuns raped. In Nigeria, churches are burned. This is being written in December 2007; last week, ten Christians were killed in Nigeria as churches were burned. Last week, fifty Muslim militants attacked a Christian church in West Java Province in Indonesia, and three Christians were killed in Pakistan. This is repeated, week after week, all over the world. While it may take a modicum of courage to get up out of a church pew and walk down the church aisle to accept Christ as your Savior in front of a crowd, that is nothing compared to worshiping in secrecy, in fear for your life and for that of your family. We honor these courageous people, wherever they are, when we remember them in our prayers.

With the exception of the categories of Punishment and Sin Happens, the other forms of suffering occur because we are Christians. And suffering for Christ occurs because we are Christians. It has elements of spiritual warfare, and the suffering occurs as a revenge casualty whereby Satan viciously attacks people who belong to God. Enlisting other believers to pray with you and for you is appropriate. It has elements of suffering to bring glory to God, and I think that everyone who has been persecuted or martyred simply because of his identity as a Christian brings glory to God. You don't have to pray that God will miraculously enable you to bring glory to God; your very sacrifice does that, in a passive sense. And likewise, praying for miraculous relief is perfectly appropriate.

This seems to be one of the purest forms of suffering, a simple cause-and-effect relationship. You are a Christian, in God's will, and you suffer purely because you are a Christian. There is no sin or deficiency in your life responsible, and there are no easy answers. Few of us in this country have ever experienced this. Death is inevitably fatal, and all of us will experience it. Suffering is inevitable, but only a few will suffer only because they accepted Christ. We who do not share in this are humbled by it, and few of us would seek such suffering. There are no quick point-and-click answers. What are we to do? Throw ourselves on God's mercy, and wait for Him to avenge us at some point in the future.

I can't come up with anything better, and apparently God didn't either, because John saw all the souls martyred for Christ under the altar in Revelations 6:9-11: "and how long, O Lord, holy and true, until you judge and avenge our blood on those who dwell on the earth?" Yet, persecution of Christians may further God's works; the persecution of the early Christians in Judea led to their dispersal, and as they fled, they took the gospel with them to spread throughout the world.

I suppose you could deny Christ and, by denying you are a Christian, spare yourself persecution. However, in Luke 12:9, we are admonished, "But he who denies Me before men will be denied before the angels of God." It would appear that there are two ways to deny Christ. The first would be to reject Him completely, in which case this verse would surely apply to the nonbeliever. So if you are not a Christian and deny Christ, you won't suffer for being a Christian in this lifetime, but when judgment day occurs, you will be denied. The implication is that anyone who would deny Christ isn't a Christian, but here the definition defines the argument. In this sense, *deny* means to deny Christ as your Savior. This is at least an honest statement of your beliefs. You deny because you do not believe.

The second way to deny Christ would be to actually believe in Christ but still deny Him, as did Peter. I am sure you are familiar with that story. In Luke 22:33, Peter says, "Lord I am ready to go with You, both to prison and to death." Yet Christ predicts that Peter would deny Him three times before the rooster crowed. By the time you get to Luke 22:60, Peter has done this. And Christ forgave Him. So at least in theory, you could be a believing Christian, deny Christ to save yourself, and be forgiven. In this sense, *deny* means that you believe in Christ, but you deny it. This is a dishonest statement of your beliefs. You believe, but you deny it.

The question then becomes, "Can I lie about my faith in Jesus Christ to save myself from persecution or death?" Peter did. And the Gospels report that Peter was supremely ashamed and "wept bitterly." So this leads us to the possibility that we could deliberately sin, be ashamed, and then be forgiven by repenting. I mean, after all, being ashamed is better than being dead. Being a live coward is better than being a dead hero, right? And Peter, once restored, became the rock upon which the church was founded, which led to the thousands being saved by preaching the gospel. Unfortunately, all Peter did was buy some time because, according to tradition, he was crucified upside down during the reign of Nero. (He requested to be crucified inverted because he felt unworthy to be crucified in the same manner as Christ.)

First, we must give thanks to Almighty God that most of us have never been put in such a position. Secondly, each person will have to make that decision for himself when the time comes. Thirdly, the only *unforgivable* sin is *true* unbelief in Christ. Fourthly, each person will have to live for the rest of his life with the consequences of making that decision and, after his life is over, will have to stand before Christ and be judged for his actions.

Sometimes there are no easy answers and no easy way out.

The Wrong "Why"

My God, My God, why have You forsaken Me?

Matthew 27:46, Psalms 22:1

Since suffering began, man has asked, "Why?" But the meaning of "why" can be many different things. In trying to work through our difficulties, it is important to spend our efforts in trying to answer the correct "why." The answer to some of our other "whys" are much more problematic and can consume a lot of our time, and the answers to many of these questions may elude us in this lifetime.

As mentioned previously, there are certain steps that must be taken before we can deal with any of our problems of suffering. Ensuring our salvation is paramount for obvious reasons, but once Christ comes into our lives, we have the Holy Spirit to teach us, and the Scriptures are unlocked to provide understanding. We can call upon God for wisdom and discernment. Baptism orients us in our first step along the road to sanctification as we begin that lifelong process of becoming like Christ. Joining into our local body of Christ gives us access to our teachers and others with knowledge and experience who can help us try and sort these things out.

Derrick was a quiet, humble young man of thirty who had lost his parents years before. I first met him when he was admitted to the hospital with chest pain. He had an ultrasound performed of his heart, which showed an enlarged aorta. This largest blood vessel is shaped like a candy cane, and it arises from the heart above the aortic valve, first ascending toward the head, where it gives off the branches to the head and arms. It curves at the top into an arch and then descends into the back of the left side of the chest and then on into the abdomen where it gives off the branches to the liver, intestines, and kidneys. Finally it splits into two branches, one to each leg.

He had been born with Marfan's disease. This is an inherited condition in which the tissues of the aorta are weakened, and the aorta dilates into an aneurysm. If the aneurysm gets large enough, it ruptures, and the patient bleeds to death. Another possibility is that the weakened aorta will not rupture but that a tear will develop in the wall of the aorta and allow blood to run down between the layers of the wall. This condition is called a *dissection*, and it can also later rupture. In Derrick's case, he had an enlarged ascending aorta but also a hugely enlarged abdominal aorta, more than four times normal. This is exceedingly uncommon in someone so young, even with Marfan's disease, yet it represented the greatest of many threats to his life.

Derrick had no one in this world. His mother had died at an early age from one of these aortic dissections. He had recently moved to the area and knew no one. He accepted all of his problems with equanimity. We decided to fix the abdominal aneurysm first, given its huge size, and planned to repair the ascending aorta in his chest later. Through a large incision in his abdomen, we replaced the aorta, beginning just below the arteries to his kidneys, and ending just above the arteries to the legs. He did fine with this surgery and was discharged shortly after. I saw him in the office afterward, and we made plans to deal with his other aortic problem in a few weeks.

Trouble struck shortly thereafter. He developed a dissection of his descending aorta in the back of his left chest. This was surprising because it was the one part of his aorta that was *not* dilated. In any event, most dissections in this part of the aorta can be treated without surgery, and we decided that we would allow this problem to stabilize for several weeks before treating the ascending aorta.

Things rapidly got worse. He developed a dissection in his ascending aorta, and then his problem was a life-threatening surgical emergency. We rushed him off to the operating room, and through an incision in the middle of his chest, we replaced his aortic valve, the aorta just above the valve containing the coronary arteries, the ascending aorta, and the aortic arch. We did all this with a Dacron graft, which is like cloth, and we even put some of this graft down into his descending aorta with plans to eventually replace his descending aorta in the future if it enlarged. This was a difficult operation, but he did well. He was sent home to recover, and again I saw him in the office, at which point he was recovering nicely. By that time, I had gotten to know him well and was impressed at how he handled ordeal after ordeal. He struggled with no one to really look after him, and he had spent much time out of work. He was eventually able to find assistance from a variety of sources and managed to get by. We arranged follow-up for several months later.

I came into work at the hospital about four months later and saw Derrick. He was on a respirator and unconscious. He was on a stretcher, traveling down the hallway to the operating room. I couldn't believe what I was seeing. I went to his side, and he was completely unresponsive. I asked his nurses what had happened. He had been driving the night before when another driver had crossed over two lanes of traffic and struck his car head-on. The other driver had a seizure disorder and had stopped taking his medication, and this had led to a seizure, causing him to lose of control of his car. Derrick didn't have a chance in the ensuing collision. He was now brain-dead, and the operating room he was headed for was not to provide him with healing. His last operation was to be as an organ donor.

Why did all these things happen to Derrick? Well, that's easy.

His health problems happened because he had an enlarged aorta. Or you could say they happened because he had Marfan's syndrome. Or because he inherited a defective FBN1 gene on chromosome 15 that directs production of fibrillin-1, which forms microtubules in the connective tissue in the wall of the aorta (I don't understand what that means, either). Or because he had difficult-to-control blood pressure that increased the stress on his weakened aorta.

He died because someone stopped taking his or

her seizure medication and had a seizure and struck his car. Or you could say he died because of a closed head injury. He died because the neurons in his brain suffered a deprivation of blood supply and oxygen, leading to irreversible cell death.

All of these statements are true and could be used to answer the question, "Why did these things happen?" These describe the *physical* causes of his death. There is another way to get at "why." Metaphysics comes from the Greek words *meta*, meaning "after," and *physika*, meaning "physics." It is really a philosophical look at the question of "why," and it can give insights into asking and trying to answer the correct "why." You see, I believe that asking, "Why is God allowing me to suffer?" may be a huge waste of time. However, asking, "Why am I suffering?" is the most crucial question of all when we are trying to diagnose and treat our problems.

In our use of the word *why*, we are usually talking about *cause* or *purpose* or *reason*. These words can have more than one meaning. For example, the "reason" something happens may be the purpose it serves, as in the *reason* I swatted the mosquito was to stop it from biting me. Alternatively, I may also use the word *reason* to mean how something happened, as in the *reason* the mosquito is dead is because I swatted it.

You will remember Aristotle from our earlier discussion of logic. He actually decided that what we refer to as "cause" had *four* meanings. If we were to look at a builder building a house, in Aristotle's system, the first meaning would be what he called the Formal Cause, and that had to do with what shape, or form, the house would take. The Material Cause would be material from which the house would be made. The Efficient Cause would be how the building was made, what mechanisms brought it together, what led to it—in this case, the builder. And the Final Cause was the purpose for which the builder built the house. What we are really seeking to find for ourselves is the Final Cause, the purpose, of our suffering.

What is crucial is to decide is which Final Cause we are seeking. When we look at the question, "Why does God allow suffering?" or, "How could a loving God let people suffer?" we are asking a general question about suffering. People have looked at this question for centuries, and some have spent their entire lives trying to figure out why bad things happen. The entire book of Job deals with a man trying to figure out why he is suffering, using the help of some "friends" with a little advice. After being admonished by God, he comes to the conclusion that God is sovereign and, he, Job, is in no position to question why God allows these things to happen. I would submit that trying to spend endless amounts of your time trying to solve the problem of how a good God can allow evil things is going to do little other than give you a headache. It's been done by many people smarter than you or I, and entire books have been written about it. It is an interesting theological problem. The specific form of the above general question is "Why would God allow me to suffer?" Trying to find the Final Cause for why God allows suffering in the general or specific case will not aid you in your efforts to diagnose or treat your suffering. And there may not ever be a discernible reason, at least not in this lifetime. And so many times people struggle and struggle to get that answer that does not and will not come. And that only *increases* their suffering.

However, finding the Final Cause for the question, "Why am I suffering?" is essential and leads us to look at each of our separate suffering categories, and that will tell us not only the purpose of our particular suffering but what we need to do try and make the best of it. The goal is to diagnose which entity of suffering is occurring in order to prescribe the correct treatment. If you have chest pain, it could be a heart attack, acid reflux, a torn aorta, a blood clot in the lungs, a ruptured esophagus, a collapsed lung, or severe inflammation of the protective sac around the heart. Or you could just have gas. It is important to know what the cause is before embarking on treatment. The sooner this is done, the sooner the right medicine can be chosen to either eliminate or reduce the suffering.

Do you remember my attempts at trying to pigeonhole suffering into some nice, neat categories? That is important, for you must figure out your own pigeonhole, the quicker the better. Just like all illnesses are not the same, with each requiring its own treatment, *all suffering is not the same*. The Final Cause yields a question that must be asked at each step along the way to diagnosis and a treatment to be applied.

Sin Happens: We live in a fallen world, and God's purpose was to apply the penalty for original sin. Such suffering is common to all of us, until God fulfills His purpose of redemption of all mankind. The question we must ask ourselves is, "Is this suffering common to all?" and the response is to not worry about it. Christ will return and make it all perfect.

Punishment: God's purpose is to exact punishment on those who do not have a saving relationship with Him. The question is, "Am I a saved Christian?" and if no, the response is to accept Christ as your Savior.

Chastening: We are outside of God's will. His purpose is to get us to return to His will. The question is, "Am I sinning?" and if so, the response is to stop it.

Pruning: God's purpose is to make us more fruitful. The question is, "Is this from God, to make me more Christlike?" and if the answer is yes, the response is not to fight God.

Spiritual Warfare: Satan's purpose is to cripple us, to revenge himself upon us, and God's purpose is to strengthen us. The question is, "Is this from Satan, to defeat me?" and the response is to fight the devil.

To Glorify God: God's purpose is to bring glory to Himself. The question is, "Is this being done so that I may bring glory to God?" and the response is to pray for a miracle that you might do so.

For Christ: Satan's purpose is to attack Christ through us. The question is, "Is this happening to me only because I am a Christian?" and the response is to pray for deliverance.

As a physician, I don't spend a lot of time worrying about why people get sick or why God allows a particular patient to get sick. They just do. However, I spend a great deal of time and energy making sure I know exactly what made my patient sick and determining what illness my patient has. The correct diagnosis is essential, for it leads to the correct remedy. If you believe you are suffering because of one reason and you are really suffering for another one, you will waste enormous amounts of time, physical energy, and emotional energy trying to deal with the problem in the wrong way. It may lead you down the wrong path, and then you will have to go back and start down the correct one. It would be nice if we could simply order some laboratory tests or X-rays that would tell us exactly what was causing our suffering; it is with the Holy Spirit as our guide that we must present our case to the Supreme Healer for Him to help us answer the correct "why?"

Part II

Complications

Excuse Me, but I Am Excused

> Then the man said, "The woman whom you gave to be with me, she gave me of the tree, and I ate."
>
> Genesis 3:12

We have so far seen how sin can lead to suffering. But can suffering lead to sin? According to early Christian teaching, the seven cardinal or "deadly" sins were lust, pride, envy, greed, wrath, sloth, and gluttony. Under certain circumstances, it would seem that suffering could lead to sins such as these:

Someone who is suffering in a bitter marriage may commit adultery.

Someone who is suffering may actually be proud of it.

Someone who has suffered misfortune may be jealous of another's success.

Someone who has suffered great financial loss may become obsessed with money.

Someone who has been wronged may become angry and seek revenge.

Someone worn down by suffering may give up on doing God's work.

Someone who has suffered deprivation may later seek to make up for such losses with excesses.

I think that one of the first things that must go through

a person's mind, either consciously or subconsciously, is the *excuse* that he makes for himself because of his sin. It is easy for us fallen humans to rationalize our sins. Many people who commit wrongs do not truly know that what they are doing is wrong. They simply lack that moral framework. Yet others who commit wrongs do so knowing that it is wrong but feel that they can justify it, and it is easier to do this by tying it in to some suffering. Your hardships give you an excuse.

God does not give us the excuse option. He gave us a list of commandments. Because you were raised in a poor neighborhood in a fatherless household does not mean that it is all right for you to steal. Because your husband is cold and demanding and drinks too much does not mean that it is fine for you to have an affair. These lessons are impossible for today's society members to digest due to the prevailing moral relativism of our times that says we are all allowed to be our own moral account managers, balancing the figures and columns as we see fit.

Unfortunately for them, God is the one who is really in charge of balancing the accounts. When we try and do it, we usurp His authority, and really, we aren't as smart as He is. Our efforts usually result in more of a mess. When I was an intern on the orthopedic service, a high-powered executive was in his office one night when he leaned his chair back and fell over and severely hurt his neck. His girlfriend fancied herself good at massage therapy and healing and spent the night with him massaging his neck. By morning, he was permanently paralyzed from the shoulders down. His suffering was made catastrophic by amateur efforts to correct it. It is best to leave some things to the experts, and I would consider God's moral expertise superior to my own.

The sin that results from our excuses and our amateur attempts at balancing our own accounts usually results in more suffering. The extramarital affair may feel good in the short term and relieve some of the pain of the bad marriage but in the long term results in a broken family, alienated children, lawyer bills, and remorse. The theft that we commit because we felt excused by our circumstances results in jail time. The envy we have over another's success eats away at us and prevents us from enjoying what we do have.

In addition, the balancing that we do usually is not very satisfactory in the long term; there is a counterfeit nature to the solution. It is like having a real debt repaid with play money. A tryst outside of marriage will never surpass the wonders of a long-term love in a committed covenant marriage. And if someone will cheat on his or her spouse to have an affair with you, they certainly can cheat on you as well. You may not have that wonderful marriage, but replacing it with a cheap substitute isn't any better, and God will not honor it.

If our efforts to self-treat our suffering cause sin in our lives to develop, it is as if we have developed complications from the side effects of our misguided efforts. As with real physical illness, sometimes the side effects of treatment can seem worse than the original problem. And sometimes side effects cannot be reversed. And if they can be reversed, you can only eliminate the side effects by stopping the treatment. They are spiritual dead ends, and you can only get out of them by stopping and turning around. Being angry over suffering caused by another (or perceived to be caused by God) will cause problems that will only go away when you stop being angry. All the excuses in the world will not make this better. It would be as if you took an antibiotic to fight a cold and got a severe rash and then said, "But I am entitled to this antibiotic! I am sick!" Okay. Keep taking the antibiotic. And keep scratching.

I am afraid I overuse our illness analogy, but some illnesses, and some suffering, is self-limited and not related to anything we did. Some illness and some suffering is self-induced. Different illnesses and different sufferings must be diagnosed so treatment can be instituted and hopefully improvement will be seen. The *correct* treatment must be applied for desired results, and the incorrect treatment will either not work or will make things worse. Self-treatment, rather than God's prescribed treatment, may lead to this, and with suffering, we rationalize self-treatment. Finally, incorrect self-treatment may result in side effects that can be reversible or permanent.

Job was in bad shape. Losing all his children and earthly possessions was bad enough without having to sit around and scrape his boils with shards of pottery. At first, Job did not sin (1:22, 2:10). And then those four quacks showed up with the wrong cures. Later, Job did sin by becoming angry and bitter (7:11, 9:18), doubtful of God's sense of justice (9:17), and perhaps even a little bit envious because the wicked prospered (12:6, 21:7). This did not make things any better and only worsened the problem. Eventually, Job had to be corrected by God, and he later repented (42:6) in order to restore his relationship with Him. So although sin did not cause his suffering, Job's suffering led to sin.

Sin can cause suffering. But suffering can cause sin, especially if we use suffering as an excuse. This sin causes more suffering. This secondary suffering all occurs as a complication of the first problem and how we deal with it. Excuses for sin do not excuse the sin, even if we use suffering as an excuse. Making an excuse before God is basically accusing Him of ignorance, as if we are telling Him something He didn't already know. He knew of your current suffering before the world began and before He wrote the rulebook. Pleading before the Judge that, "I know that I am sinning, but look at how I am (have been) suffering" doesn't work. He knows your arguments before you make them. He is not going to say, "I didn't think of that. That's awful. Of course you may sin." Save yourself a lot of misery and quit trying to outsmart God.

For Shame

> Do not let me be ashamed, O Lord,
>
> For I have called upon You.
>
> Psalm 31:17

Around sixty to eighty times a minute, your heart fills with blood and then squeezes it out. But your heart never completely empties; it only empties out a portion of the blood within. For most healthy individuals, the heart empties out somewhere between 50-75 percent of its contents. We call that the *ejection fraction.* Damaged hearts pump out less. People generally begin having symptoms when the ejection fraction is less than 30 percent, and heart failure results. Sometimes the ejection fraction falls to 20 percent, 15 percent, or even 10 percent. And sometimes these patients have serious problems with their hearts and are sent to me to see if they can be fixed. These hearts have usually been damaged by heart attacks. And the question they often ask me is, "How could my heart be in such bad shape?" They have never had any symptoms before, suffering heart damage in silence.

I don't know who is in charge in society, but somehow, sometime, someone decided that shame is a bad thing. Whoever is in charge decided that shame was a hurtful thing, something that should be avoided, and if not avoided, eliminated as soon as possible before fragile egos were damaged.

What I can't figure out is the selective nature of shame today. Based on today's culture, I have no idea what someone is supposed to feel shame over. A governor resigned for using a prostitute, but an actor arrested for using one in a car in Los Angeles continues to have a successful career. Another governor had a homosexual relationship and resigned, but a US Senator had a male prostitution ring running out of his Washington apartment, and he still has a job. And a US Representative had an affair with a seventeen-year-old male page and was re-elected six times. And a sitting United States president wasn't impeached over having sex in the White House with a young woman who was not his wife. He was impeached because he lied about it under oath.

If you have pictures of naked minors on your computer and law enforcement finds out about it, you will go to jail. But a young actress appeared naked at age twelve in the movie *Pretty Baby* as a child living in a brothel, and that is art. And an adult actress appeared in the movie *Birth* in 2004 in a bathtub with a ten-year-old boy, also making this art. If you have sex with two women at the same time, as did one young actor who was videotaped doing so in 1988, there is a scandal. But if you have sex with two thousand women, as one of our older Hollywood stars is alleged to have done, that is a magnificent scoring tally for a grand old man. I am confused. Commit a sin, apologize to the public if you need to, and then move on. Where is that sense of shame?

I am sure that most experts would disagree with me, but I believe that lack of shame is unhealthy. I am not saying that experiencing shame is a good thing, but its absence is a real problem. There are certain pathological conditions where a person cannot feel pain. This usually results in serious problems. If a person has diabetes, they may not feel chest pain when their heart is not getting a sufficient amount of blood. They can have a heart attack and not know it. These patients have a defective warning mechanism. In a healthy person who has coronary artery disease, they develop chest pain or angina when their heart muscle is starved for blood. They then seek medical attention. But those without this natural alarm system do not and may suffer severe heart damage without knowing it. By the time they do go to the doctor, they may have had several heart attacks and have only begun to develop symptoms when their heart failed. By this time, it may be too late to do anything about it.

For the purpose of discussion, I would like to separate a state of *being* from a *feeling*. Let us call the state of *being* either "guilty" or "not guilty," just as one would in our criminal justice system. And let us call the *feeling* associated with being guilty "shame." I realize that we frequently say that we *feel guilty*, but let us not use those words for our feelings.

If you sin, you are in a state of guilt, or guilty. As you stand before God, you are guilty as charged. And if you are a healthy person, you also feel shame. That shame has a purpose. It is to get you to stop your sin, repent of your sin, and ask forgiveness. You then take your sin before the Lord and confess it and repent. Once you do that, a host of miraculous things occurs. Because of Christ's work on the cross, as a believing Christian, you are forgiven. Just like that. The penalty for sin as God decreed it was death. But not only are you forgiven, you no longer have to pay the penalty for sin to God. You do not have to die. You do not have to sacrifice an animal, using its life to pay your penalty. And you now are declared "not guilty."

Because of this, the shame has served its purpose. Shame has motivated you to stop your sin, seek God, confess and repent, and ask forgiveness. Shame is no longer necessary. Like our patient with angina, whose symptom tells him that something physically is wrong and that he needs help, shame tells us that something is morally wrong and that we need to seek attention. But once we are "treated," it has served its purpose and need not be carried around forever. What we are left with is usually a sense of *regret*, which has an educational component, teaching us what we should not do again.

Let's say that you are a young man or woman and become involved in a sexual relationship outside of marriage. You are guilty as you stand before God. According to biblical standards, you *should* feel shame. This leads you to stop your relationship. You then confess your sin to God, repent of it, and ask forgiveness. You are no longer guilty. The shame has accomplished its purpose. You no longer need to feel ashamed. You may, however, always *regret* having had the relationship. And part of that regret is the knowledge that it was wrong, that you wish you hadn't done it, and that knowing better, you would not do it again.

Two obvious problems arise with a defective shame mechanism, and both increase our suffering. The first is when we have no sense of shame. And the second is when we have shame that will not leave us after God has forgiven us and it is no longer necessary.

If you don't get chest pain when you have a heart attack, then you do not realize there is something seriously wrong with you, and you do not seek the help you need. And if you do not feel shame over sin you have committed, then you will persist in that sin and not seek forgiveness. And just like the people with silent heart attacks, you will suffer progressive damage. The person who has these heart attacks suffers heart damage until they begin developing signs of congestive heart failure. And the person who continues to sin will not only continue to suffer the negative consequences of that sin, they will eventually develop congestive moral failure. Their life will become plugged up by sin. They lose their sense of moral bearing. That would seem to me why so many people with unrepentant sin in their lives in one area see it spread to other areas. The person with an out-of-control sexual issue may develop drug or alcohol problems and then financial problems. We continue in our suffering, our chastening.

It is our friend the Holy Spirit who performs the necessary function of convicting us of our sin ("And when He has come, He will convict the world of sin…" John 16:8). It is He who provides the necessary shame that motivates us to get the treatment we need. The Spirit is given to all that accept Christ as their Savior, and He comes to dwell within us, constantly pricking our conscience when needed.

But once that pricking is no longer needed, once we have confessed and repented and asked forgiveness, we do not need to continue pricking ourselves. The shame has done its work.

On the other hand, many Christians continue to suffer for sins that they have committed and for which they have been forgiven because they continue to feel shame. This is not the work of the Holy Spirit. This is largely the work of Satan.

Satan wants to immobilize you and rob you of your Christian joy by continuing to convince you that you are still guilty. People carry around feelings of shame that make them feel worthless and unworthy. This can go on for a lifetime, leading to perpetual suffering. Simply understanding that this is inappropriate and needs to stop may help someone caught up in this. If you come to me with blockages in your coronary arteries, I can perform a bypass operation on you to relieve the circulation problem. But you don't need to have that same surgery on a daily basis once the work is done.

Groundhog Day is one of my favorite movies, and *The Twilight Zone* is one of my favorite television shows, but this would be like waking every morning at 6:00 a.m. to the radio playing Sonny and Cher's "I Got You Babe" and then having the nurse come in and tell you she has to prep you for surgery.

Some people say that they just can't forgive themselves for what they have done. Well, that isn't your job. You can't do bypass surgery on yourself either. If you choose not to confess, repent, and be forgiven, well, then you *are* still guilty, and you will continue to have moral angina or shame. But if you have been forgiven, and the operation has been a success (as it always is when God is the Surgeon), then to continue to do the Holy Spirit's work of inflicting shame is wrong.

Envy

> A sound heart is life to the body,
>
> But envy is rottenness to the bones.
>
> Proverbs 14:30

If I asked you what the opposite of lost is, you would say found. Can something be neither lost nor found?

If I asked you what the opposite of black is, you would say white. Yet if something is not black or white, what is it?

If I asked you what the opposite of a hero is, you would say a coward. Yet if someone is not a hero or a coward, what are they?

Words can be funny things. The very definition of a word can change what that word includes. We can look at the meaning of words by using the terms *set* and *complement*, which you may remember from your elementary high school mathematics. A set is a collection of objects. Its complement is everything that is not in that set.

When we use the word *found*, we are referring to things that were formerly lost. If we look at the set of "lost" things, its complement is all the things that are not lost. That means things that have been found and things that were *never* lost.

When we look at the set of "black" things, its

complement is all "non-black" things, which include its opposite, white things. But if something is neither black nor white, it can be a shade of gray. Yet the complement of "black" things would include not only gray things but red ones, purple ones, green ones, and so on.

When we look at heroes, the complement of that set is "non-heroes." So if you are not a hero, you may not be a coward. You may just be a nonhero.

If the opposite of "blessed" is "cursed," must you be either blessed or cursed? Perhaps you are "non-blessed." If you are neither rich nor poor, you may be "non-rich" and "non-poor." And how do we define these words, *blessed* and *cursed*, *rich* and *poor*? We can draw arbitrary circles around our sets. But who gets to decide where that line should be drawn?

The US Bureau of the Census can divide our population into fifths, and we might consider the bottom fifth "poor." Or an arbitrary line can be drawn at some level of income in America, and we can call people with incomes below that level "poor." But what is poor in America might be well-off in another country. And few people are truly blessed in every aspect of their lives, and few people are cursed in every aspect. You can be beautiful and poor and smart and healthy, all at the same time.

Our natural fallen human nature is to compare ourselves to others. We decide which set we belong to or which set we do not belong to. And this allows for that sinful condition of envy. We covet the things that we do not have; we are envious of the people who have them. The point I am trying to make in a very roundabout way is that while we all suffer at some time, the absence of blessings is not suffering. We confuse this all the time, especially in this modern society where we are so frequently blessed and take our blessings for granted.

I am not trying to put a rosy spin on someone's suffering and say that it isn't all that bad. But as with any attempt to diagnose and treat a problem, it is important to do this as objectively as possible. As our standard of living steadily increases, so do our expectations. There were more people in America connected to the Internet at the turn of the twenty-first century than were connected to running water at the turn of the twentieth century.

Imagine for a moment that God got it all wrong, that envy was a legitimate feeling, that when you got envious you were just as justified in satisfying that desire as if you were hungry and sought food, or tired and sought rest. And imagine, if you will, that you could magically satisfy that desire. How would you feel, and what would you do? If you "suffer" from average looks but in a moment could look like George Clooney or Catherine Zeta-Jones, would you? What if looking like that brought its own set of problems, such as people thinking differently about you because of the way you looked? And how would you feel as you aged and lost your looks? What if *everyone* got their wish and looked like Clooney or Zeta-Jones? How would we feel about the words *handsome* and *beautiful?*

Maybe you are suffering from financial problems. Perhaps a million dollars would help. Would that solve all of your problems? Most lottery winners return to their previous state of happiness within one year. Would you know how to hold on to your money? It is estimated that one-third of lottery winners go bankrupt. Would you still have health worries? Are you willing to deal with all of the changed relationships with family members and friends who may expect you to share with them? And if by some magical process, what if everyone in America were given a million dollars? Given what you know about human nature, spending and saving habits, risk-taking behavior and high-flying living, how many people do you think would still be millionaires in a year's time?

Once you have determined that your basic needs for safety, shelter, food, good health, and love have been met, how much more do you really need? I am confessing that I have been guilty of having these needs met and yet still felt that I was suffering because other desires of mine were not fulfilled, and many of these desires originated in my comparisons of what I had compared to what other people had. It was the Apostle Paul who had overcome this: "for I have learned in whatever state I am, to be content: I know how to be abased, and I know how to abound" (Philippians 4:11, 12).

So I think that you have to be careful before raising the "suffering flag" that it is not just because you have not had all of your wants fulfilled. This may not really be suffering that you are experiencing. Only you can decide this, but again, this is a book about preventing unnecessary suffering or minimizing suffering, so redefining your parameters, where you draw your circle, can affect which set you are in. I hope this means more to you than simply a mental "trick" to define suffering away—a thoughtful perspective, however, is always of help.

Another way envy can aggravate suffering occurs when people who are truly suffering become envious of those who are not. In my experience, most people with true suffering have more on their minds than coveting another's good fortune—they are too busy dealing with the very real problems they face. It is also amazing how often I have seen in my practice the truly suffering person try to help others. I have had patients with terminal illnesses try to minister to other patients with problems much less severe than their own. Many of the people providing health care to the sick are suffering themselves. Still, under the influence of self-pity, we may from time to time compare ourselves with those who have not got our burden, never knowing what burden they may be carrying.

Regardless of which set we are in, envy causes a form of suffering all by itself. It keeps us from enjoying what we do have. It focuses us on what we lack, thereby depriving us of the fulfillment in other areas that we might have. Envy is never additive to our lives, only subtractive. It never gives us something; it only takes away.

I think that were it possible to envy and not sin, what we should envy is the qualities of Christ. Within seconds of your asking the question, I could immediately give you the name of someone richer than I am, better looking than I am, or smarter than I am. There will always be someone else with more than you have. Yet, sadly, within seconds of your asking the question, I could immediately give you the name of someone kinder than I am, more caring than I am, and more in the character of Christ than I am. Those are the things in life that I envy.

Unforgiveness

> And whenever you stand praying, if you have anything against anyone, forgive him, that your Father in heaven may also forgive your trespasses.
>
> Mark 11:25

In the great old movie *D.O.A.* made in 1950 (and later remade in 1988), the lead character, Frank Bigelow, walks into a police station to report a murder—his own. He has been fatally poisoned, and his time is running out. Through a complex plot, it is revealed that he was given a "luminous" toxin that damaged his internal organs; once diagnosed, he has only a few days to live. The body of the movie is Bigelow's journey to discover his killer before he dies from his poisoning.

A real-life version of this occurred in 2006. Alexander Litvinenko was a former KGB and FSB agent (the KGB was renamed FSB in 1991) who defected to Great Britain in 2000 after accusing his superiors of ordering the assassination of a Russian businessman. He later wrote two books with multiple accusations against the FSB, including bombing apartment buildings, in an attempt to help Vladimir Putin gain control of the government. On November 1, 2006, he met with two Russians in the Pine Bar at the Millennium Hotel in London, where he was poisoned with Polonium-210, a radioactive material. He became sick that day and was admitted to the hospital two days later. After three excruciating weeks, he died on November 23, knowing that he had been poisoned and naming his killers.

Most poisons work quickly, although some work over time. Throughout my career, I have seen a variety of poisonings, all self-induced. Some were with common agents, like aspirin, which works very quickly, and acetaminophen, which destroys the liver and takes some time to become fatal. Some were accidental, often from too much medication. Many were intentional. And some even required surgery. One man swallowed hydrochloric acid, and this rapidly descended straight into his stomach, where it burned a hole right through it. A young woman swallowed lye, and this took many days before her esophagus became so scarred that she could not swallow, and we later had to remove her esophagus and replace it with her colon. Although occasionally some people poison others over prolonged periods of time, most people who deliberately do so to themselves are trying to end their lives quickly. It is rare for someone to willingly take a poison that would cause them to suffer for an extended period of time. Imagine intentionally taking such a poison, one that caused much pain and waiting, and waiting, and waiting…

We occasionally suffer because of the actions of another. Sometimes people harm us unintentionally and sometimes deliberately. This can be a single event, such as an unkind word, or may be done over years, as in cases of spousal abuse. It may be as minor as temporarily hurt feelings, or it may lead to lifetime mental or physical scars. Obviously, the first priority should be to stop the direct harm, the verbal abuse, or the physical injury. And in certain circumstances, justice is required. But after that is done, we must not deliberately poison ourselves with unforgiveness.

To forgive means many things: to pardon, to cancel a debt, to cease to feel resentment. We must decide exactly what it is that we are talking about when we discuss forgiveness. To *pardon* someone is to release someone from the penalty for an offense, just as when a governor or the president pardons a criminal. When God forgives us from our sins because of Christ's sacrifice for us, He no longer will exact a penalty from us for them. The penalty for sin is death (Romans 6:23), but because Christ died for us, we do not have to do so. And if someone owes money and that *debt is cancelled*, then that debt is no longer owed. Both of these situations can apply to us when we deal with others.

For example, if someone embezzles from us, we may be entitled to both having them punished in the criminal justice system as well as having restitution made for our losses. We could forgive them by dropping the charges against them and not exacting punishment, and we also could drop our claim for restitution. Neither of these may be appropriate, for it is important for people to experience the consequences of their actions. Justice is served when the correct penalty is applied and debts repaid, although as James notes in his epistle, chapter 2, verse 13, "Mercy triumphs over judgment."

When someone has hurt us, it is natural for us to have bad feelings toward them. This is part of our fleshly nature. We may be angry with them and full of suspicion toward them. We may desire retribution. Yet this is not what God commands of us. He alone may exact vengeance (Deuteronomy 32:35). We are to "bless those who curse you, and pray for those who spitefully use you" (Luke 6:28). Even more, we are not to continue to feel badly toward them. We are to forgive them—as much as they ask for it. In Matthew 18:21 and 22, Peter asked Christ,

> "Lord, how often shall my brother sin against me, and I forgive him? Up to seven times?" Jesus said to him, "I do not say to you, up to seven times, but up to seventy times seven."

And in Luke 17:3-4, He says,

> If he repents, forgive him. And if he sins against you seven times in a day, and seven times in a day returns to you, saying, "I repent," you shall forgive him.

Well, what if he doesn't repent? Or what if someone harms you and you never see them again? Our Savior says in Mark 11:25,

> And whenever you stand praying, if you have anything against anyone, forgive him, that your Father in heaven may forgive your trespasses.

This is not conditional; He doesn't say here, "if he repents."

As a believing Christian, God does not require that we pay the penalty for sin, which is death. He has also forgiven us of our largest debt, our life. Because of this, we are to forgive others. As Paul tells us in Ephesians 4:32, "And be kind to one another, tenderhearted, forgiving one another as God in Christ forgave you." Yet we must be forgiven of our individual, daily sins, and this requires that we repent and that we forgive others. To continue in Mark 11:26, "But if you do not forgive, neither will your Father in heaven forgive your trespasses." And in Matthew 6:14, 15,

> "For if you forgive men their trespasses, your heavenly Father will also forgive you. But if you do not forgive men their trespasses, neither will the Father forgive your trespasses."

So we can see that there are three major reasons that we are to forgive: because God commanded it, because God has forgiven us of our largest debt, and because He requires it to forgive us of our ongoing sins. These reasons alone should convince us that forgiveness is essential.

But there is another reason that we must forgive, one that has to do with our final definition of forgiveness, with lessening our own suffering. We must cease to feel resentment. We must deliberately let go of those feelings and deliberately not take that poison. You see, holding a grudge is like taking poison and waiting for the *other* person to die. It eats at us and gnaws at us and continues the suffering. It is not only a poison that we can choose not to take; it is one that we can be rid of by forgiving. This can be hard to do, and it may even take some time, but it is essential to moving forward and away from the pain. If a mother loses her son to a drunk driver and never sees the driver again, she should forgive him. She should do it for the obvious reasons: that she is commanded to do so, that she should do so because God forgave her, and because God requires it to forgive her of her sins. But she should also do it because it will help her heal. It will eliminate the poison from her system. She may never forget, but she can forgive.

As long as we refuse to forgive, we will carry with us those bitter feelings. In a sense, we are handing over our chance at happiness and healing to the person who harmed us. When we forgive them, we not only release them as the object of our feelings of resentment, we release ourselves from the burden of the persistent poison. Somehow, Jacob DeShazer was able to do this after his cruel treatment at the hands of his captors. Somehow, with prayer and God's help, we must find a way do this with those who hurt us.

Angry with God

> Then the Lord said, "Is it right for you to be angry?"
>
> Jonah 4:4

I hope that this book so far has not made you feel like I am trying to preach to you. To borrow from Dr. McCoy in *Star Trek*, "I'm a surgeon, not a preacher!" And at best I am an amateur theologian. I am also not a psychologist, despite the fact that one of my undergraduate degrees was in psychology. What I guess I was put here to do is to heal, and I want to offer constructive points that will help people prevent unnecessary suffering and minimize the suffering that does occur, similar to preventing illness or at least trying to get people over their illness.

In this chapter, I want to talk about getting angry with God. This is not a discourse on anger. There are whole books on anger, other books that explain how the Christian is to deal with anger, and anger management courses and so on. But this is not that. It is about when the sufferer lets suffering make him mad at God.

Since this is a practical book, I really don't want to get into whether or not it is a sin to be angry with God. What I really want to do is to show that it is a huge waste of time.

I have heard some people say that it is okay to get angry with God; He is big enough to take it. Well, of course He is. And if Brother Bumblebee tells Brother Mosquito that it is okay to go ahead and sting me, that I am big enough to take it, he is technically correct. What Brother Bumblebee fails to tell Brother Mosquito is that I may just swat him. Nothing good comes out of being angry with God.

I am not an expert on the Bible, but I am completely at a loss to find an instance where somebody got angry with God or struggled with Him and something good came out of it. As we saw with Job, he became bitter at God and later had to repent for it. According to Hosea 12:4 and Genesis 32:24-30, Jacob wrestled with God, and all he got out of it was a name change and a bum hip with a limp for life. (Yes, although God later told him in Genesis 35:11, "…a nation and company of nations shall proceed from you, and kings shall come from your body," this was really a continuation of the covenant made long ago with Abraham.) The Israelites began complaining against Moses soon after their miraculous delivery from the pursuing Egyptians who were drowned in the Red Sea. "'For you have brought us out into this wilderness to kill this whole assembly with hunger'" (Exodus 16:2, 3). Once the Israelites started complaining against God, however, bad things began to happen. In Numbers 11:1,

> Now when the people complained, it displeased the Lord; for the Lord heard it, and His anger was aroused. So the fire of the Lord burned among them, and consumed some in the outskirts of the camp.

Eventually He sent them quail but said in verses 19-20,

> You shall eat…for a whole month, until it comes out of your nostrils and becomes loathsome to you, because you have despised the Lord who is among you.

And in Numbers 14:1-23, rebellion against God prevented the Israelites from entering the promised land—it would be only their descendants. And in Numbers 21:4-9, when, "…the people spoke against God and against Moses…the Lord sent fiery serpents among the people, and they bit the people; and many of the people of Israel died."

As we mentioned, there are whole books about anger and its effects on oneself and others. It can be a very destructive force. It is usually described as a state of emotional arousal, with your hormones surging and your heart racing, pupils dilated, body sweating, and so forth. It is characterized as a physiological "fight or flight" type of thing. And in many cases, that is so. But sometimes there is a burning anger, a sort of fuming where we have deliberately chosen an attitude and stance. Two things seem to be characteristic of this position when we become angry with other people. One is that we "build our case." Rather than seeking out what we can do to resolve the situation or look at it from another perspective, we start mounting the evidence so that we can lay out our case, our grievances, to seek redress. We go over and over the details of why this shouldn't be happening to us. A second characteristic of being angry is that we think that the sheer force of our anger and fury will cause someone to relent.

The problem with building our case is that there is no impartial arbiter between God and us. God is the judge, and what you really need from Him is mercy, not an admission of error. It is highly unlikely that you are going to be able to present some new fact or argument to God that is going to make Him say, "Well, I really didn't think about that. You're right. I will stop your suffering immediately." And while getting really angry with some people will intimidate them and cause them to give into you, it is highly unlikely that you will be able to intimidate God into doing anything. I just can't imagine God saying, "Wow. Tim is upset about this and is angry as a hornet with me. I'd better stop his suffering before he really gets mad."

So what we see is that getting angry with God doesn't really accomplish anything, whether it is an attack of fist-shaking rage or simply long-standing bitterness. Being bitter toward God, as Job was, doesn't hurt Him. It hurts us.

In many cases, this anger against God runs its course, and we see how foolish we have been. What we have done hasn't accomplished anything, and time that could have been spent constructively trying to work our way out of our situation has been wasted. Sometimes that time could have been spent identifying causes of our suffering that could have been corrected. And even if all you could have been doing for your suffering was to pray for relief, your anger has disrupted your relationship with God. And now you have to restore it.

It's just as if you have had a fight with your spouse and then realized your spouse was right. And when you fight against God, he is *always* right. (That in itself is infuriating. Couldn't He be wrong, just this once?) You have just wasted a lot of time. You haven't accomplished anything. You have disrupted the relationship. And now you have to go back and ask forgiveness to restore the relationship. With your spouse, you say, "Honey, I was wrong. Will you please forgive me?" If you are Job, you say, "Therefore I abhor myself, and repent in dust and ashes."

So go ahead; get angry with God. He can take it. But you will not accomplish anything; you will waste a lot of time; you may cause yourself unnecessary hurt and anguish by becoming bitter. If and when you come to realize that God is always right, you will have to seek restoration. Getting angry with God certainly isn't a very effective or efficient thing to do. And as you express your anger against God, you may induce more suffering. Yes, I have gotten angry with God myself. I consider myself fortunate that I have not had fiery serpents come after me or quail come out of my nostrils.

Self-Pity

> Why did I not die at birth?
>
> Why did I not perish when I came from the womb?
>
> Job 3:11

If you are suffering, in one way or another you are experiencing pain, either physical or non-physical; you *hurt.* That is a simple cause-and-effect relationship. It is a normal response, and as we have seen, those people who do not experience pain can suffer grievous injury. Likewise, it would be foolish of me to look at you in the midst of your suffering and say, "Don't hurt!" It wouldn't be possible.

Grief is similarly the response to loss. If you have lost a loved one, for me to command you, "Don't grieve!" would also make no sense. In fact, an absence of grief in a situation such as this is abnormal. Many people try to do this, however, saying things like, "He's in a better place now." That may very well be true. However, this is a book about preventing the suffering that can be prevented and lessening suffering where possible, especially by not doing the wrong things that can make it worse. It is not about reinterpreting suffering in a more favorable light. If you have suffered a loss, *it hurts*, and grief is normal. There are many forms of loss, such as a relative, a job, a home, a lifestyle, or physical abilities. To lose these things hurts. One of the most common reactions to such hurts is self-pity.

For us to discuss self-pity, we must look at the definition of what we are trying to talk about. We frequently refer to self-pity as "feeling sorry for yourself." The word *sorry* comes from the Old English word *sarig,* which means "full of sorrow." The word *sorrow* comes from *sorg*, meaning, "grief" or "regret." (These are both related to *sar,* which means "sore.") So "feeling sorry for yourself" essentially means that you are "feeling sorrow for yourself."

If *pain* or *grief* is what we experience when we undergo suffering, *self-pity* or *feeling sorry for yourself* is how we think about ourselves undergoing this process. With pain, we focus on the experience, and with self-pity, we focus on ourselves. We hurt and we feel sorrow for ourselves hurting. And I don't think there is anything really wrong about this, in the short term. If you have a friend who is in a terrible accident, you would feel sorry for them. And if you are in a terrible accident, why wouldn't you feel sorry for yourself?

I think that what is confusing is that what most people mean when they say, "Stop feeling sorry for yourself," is one of three things. They are trying to say that *what* you are feeling sorry for yourself about is wrong, that the act of feeling sorry for yourself is wrong, or that it is time for you to stop feeling sorry for yourself. Let me explain.

If you are a thirty-five-year-old man and the rubber ducky you use when taking a bath got chewed up by the dog, and your wife says, "Stop feeling sorry for yourself!" what she is really saying is that, in her opinion, losing a rubber ducky is not something that you should be upset about at all.

If you have just lost a football game, and you and your teammates are in the locker room with your heads down, and the coach comes in and says, "Stop feeling sorry for yourselves," what he is really saying is that, in his opinion, the act of feeling sorry for yourself about losing the football game is wrong—you are not entitled to it. Losing a football game may be something to hurt about, but you are not allowed to feel sorry for yourself about it. You are allowed to experience the pain but not think about yourself experiencing the pain. This is a variation of the argument I made several chapters ago, when I said, "It's not all about you."

In the first of these two cases, a judgment is being made by someone else about what something is worth to you. If your rubber ducky is one of your most cherished possessions and it is lost, then experiencing the pain and feeling sorry for yourself about it would be natural, and I am not sure that you could do one without the other. And if you are a thirty-five-year-old man who is that attached to a rubber ducky, you have much bigger problems than I can go into here.

And in the second of the two cases, someone is making a judgment over when it is permissible for you to feel sorry for yourself, even in the face of real pain. I am not sure that what is being commanded is realistically possible. Perhaps it is, for some people.

But let us look at a third case. If you have had your car stolen, you would hurt over that and feel sorry for yourself. And if thirteen years later you are still feeling sorry for yourself, then you have not moved on, and much of what is meant by saying, "Stop feeling sorry for yourself" is that it is *time* for you to stop feeling sorry for yourself. Again, someone is making a judgment over how long you may do so.

I think it is difficult for someone else to make these judgments for us. It is as natural for us to feel sorry for ourselves as it is to feel grief. The problem is twofold. The first is that an excessive amount of self-pity causes an excessive focus on ourselves. The second is that an excessive duration of self-pity paralyzes us from further action. Both of these problems keep us from living our lives out for God.

You can certainly be crippled by pain and grief. Sometimes the pain can be so unbearable that you cannot focus on anything else. Yet sometimes the pain is not so great, and it is manageable, yet we focus on ourselves so much that we do not focus on God. This keeps us from His leading and His healing blessings. Asking the wrong, "why?" or not realizing that "it's not all about me" can contribute to this excessive focus on self. You may be perfectly capable of digging yourself out of a hole. But it is unlikely that you are going to be able to dig yourself out of a hole as quickly as you could grasp God's hand and work with Him as He pulls you out.

And likewise, if you continue in self-pity past its expiration date, you make little progress. You may be very comfortable sitting there, wrapped in thoughts about yourself and doing nothing. But you are going to be sitting in that hole for a long time.

I can't tell you how much is too much or how long

is too long. You can certainly feel as much self-pity as you want, for as long as you want. But past a point, it is counterproductive. Thinking about ourselves feels good. And it is natural and unavoidable at times. But like narcotics after surgery, too much can be lethal, and taking them for too long leads to addiction.

Denial

Search me O God and know my heart;

Try me, and know my anxieties;

And see if there is any wicked way in me,

And lead me in the way everlasting.

Psalm 139:23-24

When I was training in general surgery, which is required before training in cardiothoracic surgery, there were many unusual things that we saw. One thing that always surprised us was when someone came to us with a really, really large tumor. One patient showed up with a cancer on the bottom of his foot that was so large he could not walk. Another showed up with a skin cancer on her back that was as large as a backpack, so big that she could not lie on her back. Obviously these tumors were obvious—to everyone but the person that had them.

We wondered why someone would allow something to grow so large before seeking treatment, when treatment would be so much easier and more likely to succeed if undertaken earlier. And these patients are nowhere near setting a record. The record for a tumor of the head and neck is nearly forty pounds. I believe the record for any tumor is around three hundred pounds. In an American culture that is obsessed with appearance, the norm is to worry about even the smallest wrinkle around our eyes. And a few of these normal wrinkles are enough to send some to run to a surgeon to have them surgically corrected.

But even the symptoms that we *feel* are ignored just as readily as the ones that we can see. People come to see me with lung cancer after losing *forty pounds* and coughing up blood. With a heart attack, minutes count. If you are having a heart attack, your best chance at saving your heart muscle and your life is if you get into a cardiac catheterization laboratory within ninety minutes from the beginning of your chest pain. There, cardiologists can perform an angioplasty and restore blood supply to your heart. If that doesn't work, then they may need to call a cardiac surgeon to perform emergency bypass surgery. Yet it is common to see patients a day or several days after a heart attack began. According to the American Heart Association, one of the most common reasons a person does not seek treatment for a heart attack is *denial.*

To deny means to refuse to acknowledge. If you deny something that is false, you are telling the truth. If you deny something that is true, then you are telling a lie. And as the Bible tells us, we are not to bear false witness. That means we are not to lie to others, God, or ourselves. It is possible to do all three; it is easiest, however, to lie to God and others if we first lie to ourselves. And unfortunately, it is easiest to lie to ourselves. If you lie to others or to God, without lying to yourself, then Satan must convince you to do something. If you lie to yourself, Satan must only convince you to believe something.

As with any disobedience of God's commands,

being outside of God's will for the believer results in consequences. Everyone has heard of the adage about "fooling some of the people all of the time and all of the people some of the time," but when the truth is found out, the deceiver suffers. And once credibility is lost, regaining trust is very, very difficult. One of the parts of that adage that was left out was the part about, "and you can't fool God *any* of the time." You cannot successfully lie to God. Cain tried it in Genesis, after killing his brother, Abel, when asked in 4:9, "'Where is Abel your brother?" and he replied, "I do not know. Am I my brother's keeper?"

But we can lie to ourselves indefinitely in a myriad of ways. We can deny not only tumors and heart attacks but sin itself. We can deny to ourselves facts, such as the fact we have a forty-pound tumor. We can deny that we are responsible, such as having smoked two packs of cigarettes for fifty years causing our lung cancer. We can deny the seriousness of our problem, believing that our chest pain is only indigestion. But the truth is still always there. And denying it doesn't change the fact we have a tumor, that our smoking caused it, or that we need to get to the emergency room.

We deny to ourselves because we cannot accept it. We cannot accept something that is too horrible to believe, that we may have a fatal cancer. We deny because we cannot accept the change in the image that we have of ourselves and that we want to present to others: "Why, I can't possibly be an alcoholic!" And we deny because we cannot accept what we would have to do: we would have to give up smoking or drinking, or we would have to undergo major surgery. But what if you don't have some sin you have to give up or some major surgery to undergo? Suppose you just have a *problem*? Sometimes we deny a problem because it means that what we would have to do is *ask for help*.

When you look at the twelve steps of recovery as developed by Alcoholics Anonymous, the first is, "We admitted we were powerless over alcohol." The first step in the recovery from any disease of the body, or sin, which is a disease of the soul, is to admit we have a problem. We have to break the first link of the chain, which means to set our minds free from the delusion, from the lie that Satan has asked us to believe. You may not only have to stop denying; you will likely have to stop denying that you are denying. You can't approach God for either forgiveness or help unless you admit you have a problem. If you have sinned, you have to accept that you have sinned, that your sin is not a small one, and that you will have to go to God in repentance and ask forgiveness for your sin. If you have a problem not related to sin, you still will have to admit you have a problem, that it is not minor, and that you need God's help to get you through it.

I think that most of us are guilty of some form of denial at some time. I also think that rarely is this denial complete. There is almost always something in us that doesn't feel right, that still small voice that whispers the truth to us, whether it be that there really is a problem in our life, that we may really be responsible, or that it really is serious. As painful as it may be to face the truth, whether we face it or not it is still the truth, and it won't "just go away." So what should we do? We can commit ourselves to the truth. A trusted friend may be someone we can turn to who will answer those painful questions in an honest way; we can have no more trusted friend than God. I repeat the prayer from the beginning of the chapter:

> Search me O God, and know my heart;
>
> Try me, and know my anxieties;
>
> And see if there is any wicked way in me,
>
> And lead me in the way everlasting.

Impatience

> But when you do good and suffer, if you take it patiently, this is commendable before God.
>
> 1 Peter 2:20

On January 8, 1815, the city of New Orleans was under attack. General Edward Pakenham had assembled eight thousand British troops under his command in an attempt to seize the important port city. America and England had been at war since 1812, with fighting as far as Canada and New England. Washington, DC, had been burned. And now Andrew Jackson was trying to defend New Orleans, having built up many earthen works and mounds to protect the roads into the city.

The attack began under fog in the early morning hours while it was still dark. Despite numerous attempts, the British invaders were repulsed, and General Pakenham withdrew. The English had nearly two thousand casualties, the Americans less than two hundred. Still, all of these deaths were in vain because the United States and England were not at war. A peace treaty had been signed in Ghent, Belgium, on December 24. News of this would not reach America until *February*.

In today's world, we have a very different concept of time than people did many years ago. We can instantly communicate with our friends with our cell phones and text messaging. Satellites carry nearly instantaneous messages and news around the world. You can access your bank accounts and change investments in a matter of minutes. Between microwaves and fast-food restaurants, there is nearly always immediate access to hot food. Air travel allows us to be almost anywhere on earth in less than twenty-four hours. And Federal Express can always get it there the next day. It is not surprising that our expectations have gone up and our ability to tolerate delay has gone down.

In the early 1800s, this was not true. A sailing voyage from England to the United States would take one to three months. There was no telephone, radio, or even telegraph to get messages across the Atlantic Ocean. Word that the Treaty of Ghent was signed and that the War of 1812 was over did not reach the United States for nearly two months. Travel by carriage could take weeks. Even by the middle of the nineteenth century, getting mail from Missouri to California could take nearly a month.

I include myself among modern Americans who find it difficult to wait. We have grown up in a time where a long wait for anything is the exception rather than the norm. And just as we expect instant communications and instant food, we expect instant solutions to our problems. Not only do we not like to suffer, we do not like to suffer for any length of time. We are impatient to see it end.

And here is where there may be little we can do. We may be able to prevent unnecessary suffering and reduce the suffering we experience. We do this by obeying God and not inflicting unnecessary suffering on ourselves. We cannot resist God's efforts to prune us. We can call upon God to assist us in our spiritual battles, using prayer. We get help from others. But in the overall scheme of things, we cannot get God to change His timetable. Just as getting angry with God accomplishes nothing, telling Him to hurry up doesn't do anything either.

Waiting can be one of the worst parts of dealing with suffering, almost as bad as the suffering itself. Impatience is a human flaw, but it is exacerbated by our everyday lifestyle; modern existence was not designed to satisfy the needs of patient people but of impatient ones. No one goes to the oil change place that guarantees a two-hour oil change. No one pulls up to a drive-through window that advertises itself as the slowest service in town.

One of the problems with waiting is that it seems pointless. It typically involves doing a lot of nothing. And that doesn't make sense because if you have a problem, you should be doing *something*. But when you have done all that you can do, you must turn your situation over to God and wait for Him to do what He will. And although God is not always on time (according to our expectations), *He is never late.*

While we are waiting, God is working. He has not forgotten you. You still need to pray but not to remind Him of your trouble. And He has not put your problem on the back burner to go take care of more urgent matters. God could solve your problem instantaneously. Logically, therefore, we must assume that since God does not do this, there must be a purpose for the wait. Unfortunately, one of those purposes may simply be to teach us how to wait. I am sure that at one time or another I have beseeched God to "give me patience, and give it to me now!"

Yet God is working on the problem, moving things around behind the scenes and effecting solutions. It is as if we have gone to a fine restaurant and ordered our dinner and must wait. Back in the kitchen the chef and his assistants are busy preparing our meal, and some of the cooking simply takes time. A fine dining experience will take longer than fast food.

In Genesis, we learn of the story of Joseph, who was sold into slavery by his brothers when he was seventeen. He worked for Potiphar, Pharaoh's captain of the guard, until he was falsely accused of sexual advances by Potiphar's wife and thrown in jail. He eventually was freed and became the second most powerful man in Egypt—after thirteen years. During that time, however, Joseph was not just simply sitting around doing nothing. He was continually learning and improving himself. He learned management skills by running Potiphar's household (39:5) and even when in jail (39:22). So when the opportunity came for him to manage all of Egypt (41:41), he was well prepared.

We do not know the age at which David was first anointed by Samuel. It occurred before he slew Goliath, and he was probably still a teenager then (1 Samuel 17:33 and 42). He did not become anointed king over Judah until he was thirty and king over all Israel and Judah until he was thirty-seven (2 Samuel 5:4 and 5). During much of that time, he underwent many trials and was a fugitive from Saul. These were the years that God used to form him into the man needed to rule a country.

And although Christ has been with the world from

the beginning, He did not begin his earthly ministry until He was thirty.

There are things we can do while we wait. They may not shorten the wait at all. But there are useful things to accomplish. The most important thing to do during this time is to develop our relationship with God. This is done through prayer and spending time alone with Him. He knows that you want your suffering to be over. And although the answer is, "Not now," we still must maintain our contact with Him. We must acknowledge that He is in control of our problem, and although He could solve it "just like that!" there is purpose to our waiting.

Secondly, it is important that during the wait we obtain rest. In sailing days, the Doldrums was a dreaded area near the equator between the northern and southern trade winds. This area was marked by periods of extremely calm winds, and sailing ships could be stuck there for days or weeks. We are so used to hurrying along at breakneck speed that when we are suffering in our Doldrums, we do not know what to do. One thing to do is to accept this period of inactivity and use it for rest and recovery, whether we are recuperating from surgery or temporarily unemployed. *Getting adequate rest can make all the difference in the world in our ability to tolerate suffering.*

Thirdly, we can study the Word of God. This is an active thing that we can do during our period of waiting that will assist healing and spiritual growth. As Paul stated to Timothy in his second letter (3:16),

> All Scripture is given by inspiration of God, and is profitable for doctrine, for reproof, for correction, for instruction in righteousness, that

> the man of God may be complete, thoroughly equipped for every good work.

God's instruction manual for all of our problems is found between the covers of the Bible.

Fourthly, as we have mentioned before, service to others can help make good use of our time while we wait. Time spent serving others is never wasted. It is important enough that even Christ Himself said in Mark 10:45, "For even the Son of Man did not come to be served, but to serve." I will devote a later chapter to the benefits of service.

The point is this: nothing you can do can hurry God. Being impatient does not change this. You can, however, choose how you spend your time waiting for your ordeal to be over. You can spend time with God, with His Word, get rest, or serve others. Or you can stare at the clock.

Sins of the Fathers

> For I, the Lord your God, am a jealous God, visiting the iniquity of the fathers upon the children to the third and fourth generations of those who hate me…
>
> Exodus 20:5

The Bible tells us that in some cases of disobedience that the "sins of the fathers shall be visited upon the children, even unto the third and fourth generation." How can this be, when the Bible also teaches us that we each are responsible for our own individual sins? ("Fathers shall not be put to death for their children, nor shall children be put to death for their fathers; a person shall be put to death for his own sin," Deuteronomy 24:24.) How can we suffer for the sins of another?

There is no question that diseases can be passed down from generation to generation. There are clearly inherited illnesses, like hemophilia, cystic fibrosis, Huntington's chorea, or Marfan's syndrome, like my friend Derrick had in a previous chapter. There are other diseases that run in families. There are even some heart problems that we see in families, and a strong family history is a bad sign with coronary artery disease. So physical suffering can be handed down, but how is this related to sin? This passage of genetic material would not seem to be related to sin *per se*, in that sin in an ancestor would cause genetic defects to start up and then get passed along. In fact, there was a gentleman named Jean-Baptiste Lamarck in the early nineteenth century who postulated that you could acquire a characteristic in your lifetime that could be passed on to descendants. An example of this would be a blacksmith who developed huge arms swinging his hammer having children with huge arms. That theory has been shown to be false. Inherited genetic defects causing illness would rather seem to fall under the heading of "sin happens," where sometimes bad things happen because we live in a fallen world.

But can sin be transmitted from generation to generation, causing suffering? There are two ways that I see this happening. The first is that there do seem to be some inherited tendencies. Consider Abraham and Sarah, man and wife. According to Genesis 20:12, Abraham and Sarah were also half brother and sister. When Pharaoh confronted Abraham with his desire for Sarah, in fear for his life, Abraham told Pharaoh that Sarah was his sister (Genesis 12:10-20). This was a "half-truth." Abraham did this again in Genesis 20:1-13 with Abimelech, king of Gerar.

In the next generation, in a similar situation, Isaac told another Abimelech, a Philistine king, that Rebeccah was his sister to ensure his own safety (Genesis 26:1-11). This was now a full lie.

In the following generation, the pattern is fully established, when Jacob, whose name means "deceiver," tricked his own father into giving him the blessing reserved for his oldest brother, Esau (Genesis 27). Subsequently, Jacob was the victim of a lie when his uncle promised him Rachel for a wife and then switched women on his wedding night, leading him to consummate his marriage with her sister, Leah (Genesis 29:15-30). So we see a half lie in one generation mature into a full lie in the second generation and then persist into the third generation, culminating in suffering when a lie is perpetrated onto Jacob.

So does this mean there is a genetic component to sin? This gets us into the old nature-versus-nurture argument, trying to decide if personality and behavioral traits are inherited or acquired. There is evidence of a role for both. Obesity and gluttony can be concentrated in families. Alcoholism and substance abuse also run in families, and there may be some genetic component that leads to an increased response to these things and makes one more likely to become dependent.

The other way that I see this happening is through the extraordinary influence that the parent has on the child. And a parent who lives a worldly, sinful existence will model those values for his child, who will use those means and methods to deal with life. This often creates a chain of dysfunction that continues into future generations. I have seen many families led by an ungodly parent who had ungodly children who then had ungodly children of their own. And often, each succeeding generation is worse than the one before it.

We have certainly seen criminal behavior spanning generations. And I have seen adultery in one generation passed down to sons and then to grandsons, and daughters who have been drawn to men who break their hearts. What is so often overlooked in today's society is the role of the father. If the father does not have strong moral values and does not take a role in teaching his son how to control natural male aggressive tendencies, the son may enter adolescence out of control. And we know that if the father is absent entirely, there is an increased incidence of antisocial or even criminal behavior.

The role of fathers is crucial in teaching their children how a woman should be treated. A young man learns how a woman should be treated from his father, and a young woman learns how men treat women from the same source. A boy that sees his father mistreat his mother or cheat on her will assume that is natural, and when he is grown, he will do the same to the women in his life. A girl will assume that this is how men are and will often develop relationships with or even marry men who will treat her the way she saw Daddy treat Mommy.

Regardless of whether we were handed off bad DNA in the uterus or bad role models as a child, three things are essential to remember. As we stated in a previous chapter, we are not excused. Being an alcoholic or an adulterer can be blamed on our parents, but God does hold us responsible for our own individual sins. Being a victim simply isn't allowed, and neither are these behaviors. You may call it a substance addiction or a sexual addiction, but that does not get you off the hook with God.

Secondly, God provides a remedy in His Son Jesus Christ. The curses carried across generations are broken when one accepts Christ as Savior and appeals to Him. It is His divine ability to forgive sins that was made available to all of us by His death on the cross that enables these causal chains to be broken. The individual is not only freed from the penalty of sin (death) by Christ's work, but he now has Christ actively working in his life to help free him from being controlled by sin (Romans 6:22) and the Holy Spirit to help him resist.

Thirdly, it is imperative that you not continue a chain of sin or begin one. Your children are learning by watching. How you live your life and deal with its challenges are how they will do so. They will not learn other ways until they are older. And if you live a life of moral failure, they will too, until they are old enough to either break the chain or pass the sins onto their children. *It has to stop with you.*

We may not invite the suffering brought upon us by our ancestors, but we can stop it in ourselves, and we can prevent it from being passed on, which is a lot more than we can do with our congenital illnesses. We may not be able to eliminate the portions of our DNA that control our blood-clotting system, as in hemophilia, but we can strive to eliminate as much sin as possible from our inheritance.

Part III

Asking the Physician-in-Chief

Ibuprofen, Please

> So the Lord relented from the harm which He said He would do to His people.
>
> Exodus 32:14

The following discussion is likely to make your head hurt, inflicting a little suffering of its own. It has to deal with theological issues that have troubled people for thousands of years. When a similar issue came up before, it involved the basic question of why God allows evil. And likewise, many smart people have addressed this over the centuries, studying the problem of how a completely good God and a completely powerful God can allow evil. This book does not address that issue, for it is really not helpful in solving our immediate problem. It is something that makes for an interesting exercise.

However, what I wish to discuss now is intercessory prayer. And this does have a direct bearing on our suffering. For those categories of suffering where we have not participated in bringing it upon ourselves (such as punishment and chastening), we need to petition God for relief. In cases such as Sin Happens, Spiritual Warfare, For God's Glory, and For Christ, we must call upon the Lord for His mercy and protection. This means either for the situation to change or for us to have the ability to endure the situation; in both cases, we are asking God to change something.

Where we run into deep theological waters is when we ask the question, "Does God ever change His mind?" This is a difficult question to answer, and like the problem of evil, it is probably best not to spend enormous amounts of time on it, leading to confusion in the midst of suffering. However, for us to pray for deliverance from our suffering, we do need to know exactly what it is that we are trying to accomplish. Are we trying to get God to change His mind about what He is allowing to occur in our lives?

Imagine that you are standing on the very tiptop of a tall mountain. If you are indeed at the very apex, then a step in any direction will be a step down compared to where you are. Likewise, if something is perfect, as we define perfect, then any change will mean a step away from perfection. If God is perfect, then any change is a step away from perfect. And if God's will is perfect, then any change to that will is a step away from perfection, or it implies that the original will was not perfect to begin with. This is why it is so difficult to accept that God, Who knows all things, including future events, could ever change His mind.

Let us divide time into that which occurred up until the last chapter in the Bible, when the Apostle John gave us the inspired Revelation. Prior to that time, God spoke to man through a variety of means, including directly and through prophets. And there were many times in the Old Testament when God appeared to change His mind. There were chiefly three different manifestations of this. The first was when God seemed to regret something He had done, such as when he was "sorry that He had made man on the earth, and was grieved in His heart" over the creation of man prior to sending the great flood (Genesis 6). This indicated God had changed His mind about how He regarded something He had already done.

The second involved *conditional* statements, where a choice was offered. When God sent Jonah to Nineveh, He stated that if the citizens of Nineveh repented and turned from their evil ways, He would not destroy them. This does not truly indicate a change in God's mind; He simply lays out alternative possibilities depending on the response of the people. However, if the people of Nineveh did *not* repent and change their ways and God did not destroy them, or if the people repented and God *still* destroyed them, then that would represent a change in His plans. In the Bible, when God offers people choices with consequences, these conditional statements, He follows through.

However, the third manifestation appears to involve a clear change of plans. God tells someone what He is going to do, and then He is petitioned to change His plan and does so. When the disobedient Israelites offended God by debauchery and creating the golden calf (Exodus 32), He told Moses that He intended to destroy them. And Moses interceded for them, and God did not do so. This appears to be an instance where God truly changed His plans based on the intercession of man. And this causes conflict with our notion of an unchangeable God.

If God states a plan and is petitioned to change it and does, then we are left with two conclusions. One is that God did indeed change His mind. The other possibility is more unappealing—that God was dishonest with us. This would mean that He knew all along what He was going to do, that He knew what His final decision was going to be, and that He did not tell us the truth about His plans. But we know from Scripture that God does not lie or change. We learn in Numbers 23:19 that:

> God is not a man, that He should lie, nor a son of man, that He should repent. Has He said, and will not do? Or has He spoken, and will He not make it good?

People have tried to argue against this sack of problems in a variety of ways, chiefly by bending words. One way to handle this is to say that God's character never changes but the way He deals with us changes based on our response to Him. That may be true but still means that He can change His mind—just not His character. Another way to deal with this is to say that God's stated plans to us often are *unstated* conditionals, without our knowing it, meaning that what God is really going to do depends upon what we do. This still leaves us with an inconsistency between what God says He is going to do and what He actually does. A third argument that has been proposed is that God threatens man to get him to do what He knew was going to happen anyway. That sentence makes my head hurt a little right now. This would mean that in the case with the Israelites, God threatened them with destruction, which He knew was not going to happen, in order to get Moses to intercede for them, which He knew was going to happen, so that the Israelites would be spared, which was the plan all along. This also seems somewhat dishonest. And there are several other arguments made to basically claim that God didn't and doesn't change His mind. We will try and resolve this problem in the next chapter.

More Ibuprofen, Please

> And also the Strength of Israel will not lie or relent. For He is not a man, that He should relent.
>
> 1 Samuel 15:23

In our last chapter, we looked at many of the confusing questions that arise when we petition God for a change in our lives. We have seen that there is a seeming contradiction between a perfect God with a perfect will and perfect knowledge of the future, Who states a plan to us and then is willing to let that plan be changed. Like many theological questions, there is no easy answer. As we have seen, another difficult problem to settle is that of how a loving God could allow suffering in the first place. If God is all-loving, then He would never allow suffering, would He? Yet He does, so then He must not be all-powerful, right? These types of questions seem to embrace apparent contradictions.

What we have been doing is addressing our apparent need to have God change His mind, to do something that He would not otherwise do without our petition, in order to stop our suffering. What I am about to suggest is not an answer but a solution and an explanation for that solution.

It will not provide easy answers to the questions of the previous chapter.

Since the time of John and God's last written Word

to us in the Bible, when God spoke directly to John, there has been a shift in His manner of communicating to us. Prior to that time, God spoke directly to man, through visions and through His prophets, among other methods. As we discussed in the chapter on knowing God's will, He now speaks to us by the Holy Spirit through prayer, circumstances, the church and fellow believers, and His Word. What God does not reveal to us is His sovereign will before it happens. We do not know in advance what God plans for us as individuals, communities, or nations. That knowledge is only available in hindsight. We know of the end times and the second coming of Christ, but other than that, all we know of God's sovereign will is history. Through prayer and probabilities, supplication and statistics, we can make efforts to predict the future, but we can *never* know what God's sovereign will is for us. What we can know is His moral will—what He desires for us, what He wants us to do, and what He commands us to do—but we cannot know His plan for us.

You see, although God clearly communicated His intentions to those men in the Bible, He does not do so with us. He does not clearly state to you that it is His plan that you will lose your job and stay unemployed, or that your spouse's lung biopsy will be cancer, or that you will stay in prison endlessly because you are a professed Christian. So we pray for a job, a benign diagnosis, or release from our captivity. We know where we have been and where we are, but we do not know where we will be. I would therefore submit to you that we do not need to know whether or not God can change His mind. We do not know what His plan for us is. And in these situations, we are commanded to pray.

Jesus instructed us in prayer. He gave us the Lord's Prayer, with petitions for our daily bread, forgiveness, and deliverance from temptation. Jesus Himself prayed for deliverance. And although Jesus knew the will of the Father, we do not. And as so many people have said before me, the purpose of prayer is not to change God but to change us. We are to pray in the name of Jesus, which means to pray in the will of God. We are to align our will with that of God so that we will pray for those things that He desires to give us (1 John 5:14).

At the turn of the nineteenth century into the twentieth, a scientist named Edward Thorndike put cats into homemade puzzle boxes to see how they learned to get out. To successfully get out, the cats would need to pull on a wire loop, or press a lever, or move a bar. The cats would try a way out, and when that didn't work, they would try something else. They would keep trying until they got it right. Thorndike called this "trial and accidental success" learning, but ever since then it has been known as "trial and error." In many ways, we are like the cats in the boxes, seeking the correct way out. And it is not known to us in advance, nor do we have the understanding of the Creator. Since we are to have our will molded to be more aligned with the will of God, it would superficially seem that our prayer life is like that of the puzzle-box cats, continuing to offer up prayers in a trial-and-error fashion until we get it right.

Eventually we have enough learning successes that we ask for the things that God wants to give us.

However, such a view would suggest that the older and more spiritually mature that you are, the further down the road of sanctification that you are, the more your prayers would be in line with God's will and the more likely that it is that your prayers would be answered. Your batting average should go up. It would suggest that fervency has little effect, that simple intensity of desire is secondary to correctness. It would suggest that recruiting more people to pray for you would be of minimal added benefit, for if the crowd is praying for something that is not in God's will, a lot of incorrect prayers won't do any better than one incorrect prayer will.

We have something that those cats didn't. We have something that isn't talked about much in sermons or books these days. In fact, what we have isn't even mentioned in the Bible very much. *God* is mentioned in the Bible 4,773 times. *Jesus* is mentioned in the Bible nearly 1,000 times, and that doesn't count the Old Testament prophecies about Him. But the Holy Spirit is mentioned in the Bible only 450 times. And He is our key. Jesus is our intercessor with God (Romans 8:34). He presents our case to the Father. We have to approach the Father through the Son. But it is the *Holy Spirit* that guides us in prayer. Frederick Dale Bruner referred to the Holy Spirit as "the shy member of the Trinity." And the Spirit hardly gets any attention compared to God and Jesus. He teaches us all things (John 14:26) and prays for us with "groanings which cannot be uttered" (Romans 8:26). I see little of the Holy Spirit written about today or preached from the pulpit, and we sing a lot of hymns about God and Jesus, but when is the last time you sang a song about the Holy Spirit? I often think that this is because we are concerned about what the rest of the world would think about us dealing on a regular basis with the supernatural. And the Holy Spirit never draws attention to himself, only to Christ.

The Holy Spirit is critical to our prayer life, which is then like *coached* trial-and-error learning. The Holy Spirit is our coach. We have the Spirit to guide us in our prayers, to mold us and our will, and to bring us into alignment with the will of God so that we pray for the things He wants to give us. We offer up prayers to God with the guidance of the Holy Spirit Who leads us in what to pray. I think that we should not worry about getting God to change His mind for us. We don't know what His mind is. If we changed God's mind, we wouldn't know it! We don't know His sovereign will in advance. It may be that He has planned that you will die of lung cancer. It may be that He has planned that you will be healed. Whichever happens, we cannot know which would have been God's will for us.

We can construct thought experiments to challenge our views of God. Can a God Who is all-powerful make a square circle? Can a God Who is all-powerful create a stone so heavy He cannot lift it? These are old conundrums. I do not believe that questions such as these enlighten us. Can a perfect God with a perfect will change His mind and still be perfect? I do not believe that this is something that we should be concerned about. Not knowing God's will, we are to still pray.

We are still to petition Him. We are to be obedient in that regard. The Bible is full of instructions to pray. Jesus Himself would not have prayed in Gethsemane if He had thought it would be futile. Sometimes we must pray fervently (James 5:16), and in that garden, Jesus prayed until his sweat was like blood. And we are to pray with other believers, for corporate prayer is important (Matthew 18:19). We pray in all of our sufferings because we are commanded to. We pray in many of our sufferings because there is nothing else we can do *except* appeal to God. It is our *only hope.* And in a fallen world where sin happens, where Satan attacks us, and where Christians are persecuted, answered prayers always represent a miracle.

Unanswered Prayer

> O Father, if it is possible, let this cup pass from Me.
>
> Matthew 26:39

We went through a lot of headache-inducing problems in the last two chapters in order to try and see why it is that we pray and what it is that we are trying to accomplish. We are not to worry about changing God's mind, for we cannot know what that is. We are to pray for our needs, and sometimes that is a resolution to our suffering, and sometimes that is a change in our capacity to endure it.

But what if we are believing Christians with a saving relationship with Jesus Christ, and we petition, and that petition is denied? Then there are five logical possibilities. The first is that intercessory prayer does not work at all.

A second possibility is that we did not have enough faith or feel that we did not pray fervently enough.

The third possibility is that our prayer was not heard. This may happen when there is unconfessed sin in our lives, or sin that we have yet to repent, that is separating us from God. Our connection with Him is broken. We must search for these spiritual blocks in order to have effective petitions.

A fourth possibility is that the intercessory prayer was done incorrectly. Jesus Himself stated that "whatever you ask in My name that will I do" (John 14:13). This has generally been interpreted to mean that we must ask in such a way that what we are requesting is in the will of God. And yet Jesus prayed for deliverance in the garden of Gethsemane and was denied. If Jesus cannot pray in Jesus's name and get results, how are we to do it?

The final possibility is that the intercessory prayer was asking for something that God does not want us to have. And this is what we generally assume, that we have been asking for the wrong thing. But in all of these cases, we are assuming that praying to God is worth doing, or else all throughout the Bible, people would not petition Him and we would not be commanded to do this very thing.

This very real problem of unanswered prayer causes much suffering to add to what we already have. Sometimes people aggravate their suffering by endlessly questioning themselves and what it is that they have done to warrant such misery, never ceasing the spiritual gut check. And likewise, people struggle with self-doubt when their prayers are not answered. I cannot tell you how many patients' families have struggled with guilt and self-recriminations when their prayers for their loved one to survive were not answered. I have heard them say, between their sobs and tears, "Well, I guess we just didn't pray hard enough," or, "I guess I just didn't have enough faith."

Some of the same approaches that we have used to assess and evaluate the causes of our suffering can be used in the same manner to try and figure out why our petition is denied.

You had best have access to the Father through the

Son. Jesus is our intercessor, our priest, and it is He who enables us to approach God with our needs. Just as we avoid punishment by having a saving relationship with Christ, that same relationship allows us to come to the Father through the Son (John 14:6).

As with chastening, we must ask ourselves if we are in God's will. If we are out of His will and do not correct that situation, then it is unlikely that God will put an end to the suffering. If you are in an adulterous relationship and continue outside of God's will, then praying for your marriage to not be so miserable is not your first priority. Confessing and ending your sin is. In addition, unconfessed sin in our lives disconnects us from God. Whether we are praying for ourselves or another, we must search our hearts and carefully seek to know if there is anything that needs confession or repentance in order to restore us to that open relationship with God. We must do a spiritual gut check.

Sometimes it is not all about you. You may be a believing Christian, in God's will, with no unconfessed sin, yet your prayer is unanswered. You have to remember, God is working out His purposes, not yours. If you have a loved one in the intensive care unit, you pray continuously for him, and things don't work out well, you may have to consider the possibility that there was absolutely nothing wrong with you or your prayers. There is nothing for which you should be ashamed.

Let us look at the last two of our logical possibilities, that the prayer was not done correctly or that we asked for something that God did not want us to have. As we saw in previous chapters, these are somewhat related.

Our goal is to pray, "in Jesus's name," which generally has been interpreted to mean that we pray as Jesus would, in the will of the Father, and try to align our will with that of God so that we will pray for the things that He desires to give us. We have the Holy Spirit to guide us in this endeavor. If we were perfectly sanctified, then we would have a will perfectly aligned with God, and we would never ask for something that He would not desire to give us. And presumably, all of our prayers would be answered and we would bat a thousand. But we are not perfect or perfectly sanctified, in this lifetime, and our wills are not perfectly aligned with God's. This is not a problem we can fix immediately. We can only hope that, over time, with the Holy Spirit as our guide, through prayer, we will be molded into that perfect shape.

Let us return to our old bugaboo, logic, and talk about necessary and sufficient conditions in order to evaluate faith and fervency. A necessary condition is one that is required for something to happen. If you want to make a cake, you must have flour. Flour is a necessary condition to make a cake. A sufficient condition is one that will result in a particular outcome with nothing else required. If you fall out of the boat into the lake, you will get wet. Falling out of the boat is all that it takes.

But as you can see, other things may be required to get a desired outcome besides the necessary condition. To make a cake, you also need eggs, butter, sugar, and so on. In fact, each of these is a necessary condition. And with a sufficient condition, that may not be the only way to achieve an outcome. You can get wet by taking a shower, by standing in a rainstorm, or by diving into a pool.

I believe that when Jesus was talking about having faith as small as a mustard seed moving a mountain (Matthew 17:20), He was talking about a necessary condition. When the apostles approached Him after unsuccessfully trying to cast out a demon, He faulted them for "the littleness of your faith." He told them that "if you have faith the size of a mustard seed, you will say to this mountain, 'move from here to there,' and it will move; and nothing will be impossible to you." This has usually been taken to mean that we do not have adequate quantities of true faith. In fact, this would suggest that *no one* has had that much faith because no mere mortal human has yet convinced a mountain to move by speaking to it. Wouldn't it be great if we could find such a person? We could get them to pray to end all cancer, stop all wars, or at least put an end to taxes, all things that we have been unable to accomplish. If having true faith the size of a mustard seed were a sufficient condition, then if anyone had it, all these things could have been accomplished. Alternatively, because these things have not been accomplished, no one has had that much faith.

Well, you could say that what you wanted to accomplish was not as big as moving a mountain, that all you wanted was a new car. Maybe you could get that with a faith that was a fraction of the size of a mustard seed for that request. But what I believe Jesus was trying to state was that this faith was a *necessary* condition. You have to have that kind of faith to move mountains. But it may be that this is not a sufficient condition, that it alone is all that is required. There must be other conditions as well. I think that most importantly, what you are trying to accomplish with your prayers must be in God's will. This is another necessary condition. If what you are praying for is not in God's will for you, you could have faith the size of Antarctica and get nowhere. The apostle Paul asked God three times to remove the thorn from his side; I presume Paul was not lacking in faith in the slightest. Jesus Christ Himself prayed in the garden of Gethsemane that He be spared the divine wrath of God. He prayed in Luke 22:42, "Father, if it is Your will, take this cup away from me"; in fact, he prayed to the point that "His sweat became like great drops of blood falling down to the ground." Well, you can't get more fervent than *that.* I don't think Christ lacked in faith or fervency. As Christ put it, "if it is Your will," and later, "nevertheless, not My will, but Yours, be done." Christ submitted Himself to His Father's will because that is the more important condition—it overrides everything else.

We are not perfect, and we do not know God's perfect will. God does not expect us to offer perfect prayers, full of perfect faith and fervency. He expects us to pray the very best we can, seeking guidance from the Holy Spirit.

Decisions, Decisions

> So let the gods do to me, and more also, if I do not take your life as the life of one of them by tomorrow about this time.
>
> 1 Kings 19:2

A man prays over a job offer, accepts it, and it turns out to be a painful and unpleasant job.

A man prays over a large purchase, makes it, and it turns out to be a lemon.

A church prays corporately over purchasing some land, does so, and a year later finds itself in debt.

A patient and his family pray over whether or not to undergo surgery, proceeds, and things don't work out very well.

I have been a part of all of these.

Have you ever made a bad decision? If you told me no, I wouldn't believe it. Have you ever prayed over a decision, followed the Lord as you felt He was leading you, and things still didn't work out right? Don't answer yet. Wait until the end of the chapter.

If you recall from chapter 14, we talked about hearing God's voice. We talked about God communicating to us by the Holy Spirit through His Word, the church and other believers, life circumstances, and prayer. We talked about hearing from false sources—the world, the flesh, and the devil. And in asking God the correct "why," the spiritual gut check, we try to determine the cause of our suffering so that we can change what we have to and pray for what we need. And God will never lie to us if we sincerely seek His wisdom on these matters.

But what about when we need to make decisions? What if our prayerful decision results in suffering?

Elijah was a prophet of God. In 1 Kings his story is told. In chapter 17, God instructs Elijah to proclaim a drought to Ahab, king of Israel, because of the national sin of worshiping other gods. This lasted for three and a half years. Elijah then went to Ahab and told him to gather all *his* prophets and all the people of Israel on Mount Carmel. There Elijah challenged Ahab's prophets who worshipped Baal to see which God could light a fire under a bull; "…the God who answers by fire, He is God" (v. 24). The heathen prophets called on Baal to no avail. Elijah doused his bull and altar with water and then called upon the Lord, and fire came down and consumed the bull and the altar and the stones and the dust. This incited the people of Israel, and they chased all the prophets of Baal down to the Brook Kishon and killed them, all 450 of them.

Ahab's wife, Queen Jezebel, then swore to Elijah that she would have him killed (19:2). He ran for his life and into the wilderness. He finally sat down under a tree and "prayed that he might die, and said, 'It is enough! Now, Lord, take my life, for I am no better than my fathers'" (19:4).

So here is a guy who is following God's instructions, who is now suicidal and praying for death. If you prayed for God's direction, followed it, and were then fleeing for your life, how would you feel?

George Mueller was a nineteenth-century English evangelist with a heart for orphans, helping to provide care for nearly ten thousand of them through his ministry. In his writings, he described a process for determining God's will when making decisions.

1. I seek at the beginning to get my heart into such a state that it has no will of its own in regard to a given matter.
2. Having done this, I do not leave the result to feeling or simple impression. If I do so, I make myself liable to great delusions.
3. I seek the will of the Spirit through, or in connection with, the Word of God.
4. Next, I take into account providential circumstances. These often plainly indicate God's will in connection with His Word and Spirit.
5. I ask God in prayer to reveal His will to me aright.

6. Thus, through prayer to God, the study of the Word, and reflection, I come to a deliberate judgment according to the best of my ability and knowledge[4]

What if you do all of these things and yet your decision still results in suffering?

When we seek direction from God in prayer and things still work out wrong, there are three logical conclusions. The first is that there is a problem with us, that we did not correctly interpret what God wanted us to do. As mentioned, there are many things that can interfere with our ability to hear God clearly, including unconfessed sin and the competing communications from the world, the flesh, and the devil. We talked in a previous chapter about how we can try to avoid some of these faulty messages. The second possibility is that God lied to us. I'm pretty sure that we can discard that one. So if we didn't hear the message wrong, or the message wasn't wrong, then…

Everyone familiar with the Bible knows the story of when Jesus calmed the waters. In Luke 8:22-25, the disciples are in a boat on the Sea of Galilee when a storm comes up. Their boat is filling with water, and "they were in jeopardy." Jesus was sleeping, and they awoke Him, saying, "Master, we are perishing!" And Jesus stopped the storm, and the disciples marveled that even the winds and the water obeyed Him.

But go back to verse 22: "And He said to them, 'Let us cross over to the other side of the lake.'" They were in the boat, in a storm, their lives threatened, and Jesus had told them to get in the boat!

The most dangerous place for a Christian is to be out of God's will. But you can be smack dab in the middle of God's will and still be in a world of hurt. You can prayerfully seek His guidance, receive the correct message, be obedient, and still suffer. And if God is not wrong, the message is not wrong, and we do not hear the message wrong, then...

We should obviously pray then plan, not plan then pray. But if we have done everything correctly and still things don't work out well, then the third logical conclusion is that *this is the way it is supposed to be.* This is very, very difficult to accept. When performing heart surgery, there are many decisions to be made before, during, and after the operation, and all of these are open to error. We must evaluate each patient and his ability to tolerate the procedure. We must choose the correct procedure. And in carrying out the operation, essentially every stitch is a decision—where to place it, how to do it. And still sometimes things don't work out.

We prayerfully seek God's guidance. And if we genuinely seek Him and are obedient to what we hear, then when things come out wrong they really came out right. This is our third possibility. No matter how wrong they seem to us, they are right in God's eyes. Isaiah 55:9 says, "For My thoughts are not your thoughts, nor are your ways My ways, says the Lord." Just as we cannot keep endlessly performing the spiritual gut check, we cannot endlessly torment ourselves over decisions that were prayerfully made. God has a larger plan than we can envision, and you never know how that plan will ultimately work out. In Elijah's case, God comforted and supported him in his time of need and ultimately took him to heaven without experiencing death. In the case of the disciples, Jesus manifested his power over nature and calmed the storm. In my case, I was offered a job in another city, where I would be able to utilize my talents to their fullest. I prayerfully considered this offer, and felt God's leading to accept. I left a wonderful job and church family to relocate. Soon after, the job became very unpleasant and much grief followed. I began to seriously question my decision and whether I had truly followed the Lord's calling. It was in that city, however, that I met my future wife. After we were married, I took a far more rewarding position. As I looked back and wondered how I could have been so wrong at choosing to take that job, I realized that I hadn't been wrong at all. It was where God brought me Carol, who has been the greatest earthly blessing I have known.

Part IV

Other Prescriptions

Mundane Miracles

> The things which are impossible with men are possible with God.
>
> Luke 18:27

So this guy gets caught trying to get away during a flood, and as the floodwaters are rising, his foot gets stuck under a huge tree trunk. The water is rapidly rising and soon is up to his waist.

Two men in a rowboat come by and offer to help him out. They throw him a life preserver attached to a rope, and one of them calls out, "Grab a hold, and we will pull you out!"

And the trapped man replies calmly, "No, thank you. I need no help from you. I have faith in the Lord. He will save me."

So they go on their way.

A few hours later, the water is up to the guy's neck. And another group of guys in a rowboat come by and offer to throw him a line.

And the trapped man replies calmly, "No, thank you. I need no help from you. I have faith in the Lord. He will save me."

So they go on their way.

A half hour later the water is up to the guy's nose. And a helicopter flies over and drops a rope ladder. One of the pilots yells down, "Grab a hold, and we'll pull you up!"

And the trapped man replies again, "No, thank you. I need no help from you. I have faith in the Lord. He will save me."

So they go on their way. And the man drowns.

He arrives in heaven steamed. He can't believe it. And he storms down the hallway to God's office, bangs on the door, and barges in past God's secretary. He walks up to God and says, "What happened?"

And God says, "What do you mean?"

And the man says, "I had so much faith in you! I truly believed in you and your miraculous ways. I have had towering faith in you since I was a child, never doubting you and your omnipotence. When others around me were weak in their faith, I was strong. And you let me down. You let me drown. How could you do this?"

And God says, "I don't know what more you could want. I sent you two rowboats and a helicopter."

So often we expect help from God in the way we want it, when we want it. Many times we ask for what we would term a *miracle*. The nature of miracles has been debated for thousands of years. Before you can decide whether or not miracles occur, you must agree upon what constitutes a miracle. And to do that, you must agree upon what constitutes the law of nature. And it helps if we start with a definition of naturalism.

Naturalism is the philosophical belief that the *only* thing that is real is what we see in nature. Therefore, anything outside of nature is not real. This means that there is nothing supernatural, such as God.

The "law of nature" means that this is the set of rules that we can use to define how nature operates. Imagine, if you will, that the entire universe was a football game in a stadium. The law of nature would be the rules of the football game. Naturalism would deny that there was anything outside of the stadium. In our real universe, the laws of nature would include things like the law of gravity, the laws of thermodynamics, and so forth. You don't have to believe in naturalism to believe the law of nature.

And both naturalists and people who believe in the supernatural have come to generally define a miracle as anything that violated a law of nature. An example would be something of heavy mass that floated, or a burning log in the fireplace that steadily grew in size rather than deteriorating into ash. It is interesting that man has been able to use the laws of nature to his advantage. We can create a rocket that uses the laws of thermodynamics and a fiery combustion of fuel to overcome the *effects* of gravity here on earth, but that does not violate the *laws* of gravity. Yet if a bowling ball floated in midair here on earth with no support, that would violate a law of nature. And that would be a miracle. And most people would say that it would require something outside of nature, something supernatural, to intervene to break that law. The naturalists would believe that to be impossible, and the Scottish philosopher David Hume would argue that it would make more sense to believe that someone seeing the bowling ball floating had either imagined the whole thing or lied about it, rather than it had actually happened.

The philosophical argument between the naturalists and supernaturalists has raged for a long time, with each side trying to prove its point. I will not go into all of these arguments. But if you accept the existence of God, He is supernatural and outside the framework of nature. In fact, He *created* nature. And even the people who have accepted the existence of God as the creator of nature—the universe, our world, and everything in it—have disagreed over whether or not God actually intervenes to change things in it.

What I would say next would get me kicked to the curb by any decent philosopher. I would argue that if what you start with is nothing and you end up with our universe and world and our life and our bodies, that in itself is a miracle. If you start with absolutely nothing, the law of nature for that system is *nothing*. Nothing generates nothing, and nothing comes from nothing. So for something to come from nothing, the natural law of that system had to have intervention, or a miracle. In addition, if you remember our discussion from the very first chapter, one of the laws of nature is the second law of thermodynamics, which states that usable energy eventually becomes unusable energy; things run down, deteriorate, and disorder replaces order. So, to me, it would seem that if this is a law of nature, then anything that violates that would be a miracle.

I use a pretty liberal idea of miracles. Just like a young child that puts a coin into a vending machine and sees it miraculously converted into a soda, I see miracles in the everyday things we take for granted. And things we consider routine in our lives today would seem miraculous to people a few hundred years ago.

A Boeing 747 weighs 870,000 pounds. To see one of

these things floating and moving in midair would seem like a miracle to someone in 1808. To hold a small plastic device to our ear and speak to someone on the other side of the world would seem a miracle to someone in 1908. To give someone a medicine that would put them to sleep and prevent them from feeling pain while someone cut them open would have seemed a miracle to someone in 1808, extraordinary in 1908, and a routine part of surgery in 2008.

Two hundred years later, I see miracles every day. I split people's chests wide open, give them medicines that prevent their blood from clotting while on the heart-lung machine, stop their hearts, cut their hearts open, and rearrange their anatomy. Then their hearts start back up again, we stop the machine, we give them another medicine that makes their blood clot again, and close them up. And in routine cases, they go home a few days later. The hole in their chest had been big enough for me to get my hands into. In a battle, such a hole would have been fatal. In nature, had such a hole occurred, say by a fall or injury from a vicious animal, it would have been fatal. Yet it heals with only a thin scar to remind these patients. Strictly speaking, I have not violated the law of gravity or a law of thermodynamics, but the fact that their hearts start beating again, their blood clots, and the wound heals is always a miracle to me.

If I took my operating team and equipment back in time to fourteenth-century Europe and performed heart surgery, we would either have been worshiped or burned at the stake as witches. But today we look upon heart surgery as a routine thing. If you had a blocked-up heart valve a hundred years ago, you died. Today you can have that valve replaced and live normally. If I could have given someone that heart valve a hundred years ago, it would have been looked upon as a miracle. If you had a blocked-up heart valve a hundred years ago and prayed for healing and it went away, it was a miracle. Today, if you have a blocked-up valve and you get it replaced with heart surgery, it is no big deal. Should the person whose condition was fatal and is now healed be any less grateful to God? Is it really any less of a miracle?

What does this have to do with reducing suffering? The point I am trying to make is that sometimes we need a "real" miracle, a real violation of the laws of nature. As a heart surgeon, I see these occur from time to time. I have seen many patients who have had absolutely no chance of survival pull through, both in the operating room and afterward. Jesus didn't have antibiotics, corneal transplants, or transfusions; His healing of the lepers, the blind, and the woman with bleeding required a supernatural miracle. These people approached Jesus with their problems; likewise, we must seek a miracle by prayer to the Almighty.

But everyday miracles are also at hand. They are also a gift from God. The X-ray that finds the problem, the drug that works, the surgery that heals are modern-day miracles. And we must use these as well, realizing that they come from God, as does all healing. Most of our suffering will be alleviated by the everyday miracle, not the dramatic ones. They requirc patience. We should not overlook the mundane in favor of the divine because the former comes from the latter, and we should not give up hope because a divine solution has not occurred—a mundane miracle may suffice as well.

Suffering at the End

> Since his days are determined,
>
> The number of his months is with You;
>
> You have appointed his limits, so that he cannot pass.
>
> Job 14:5

I perform very high-risk heart surgery on a regular basis. The *average* age of my patients is seventy-four years old. My surgical results are good, but a few patients under my care will die each year. Most of these patients have exhausted all other options, with failing hearts that can no longer keep them going. And people in this situation are desperate. They usually assume that if they have the surgery they will be dramatically improved. They also accept the alternative that they will have the surgery and die. That usually does not bother them, for two reasons. The first is that their life is so miserable that they feel like they can no longer continue to live in that fashion. The second is that they are certain that they will die without the surgery. They commit the logical error known as the false dilemma. They assume there are only two outcomes: that they will have the surgery and do great or have the surgery and die quickly.

There is a third outcome, which is that they survive the operation but have complications. They have a stroke or respiratory failure or kidney failure or something like that. They come through the operation well, but in their weakened condition, they require prolonged intensive care. And this is terrifying because no one wants to live like that. No one wants to buy into extended suffering deliberately. Our society believes in death with dignity.

We even have death-with-dignity laws. I think that is just junk.

Making end-of-life decisions is difficult for any person with a serious illness, not just those who have had heart surgery. People become critically ill every day. What I am about to propose goes entirely against the grain of our modern society and modern ethical thinking and will be rejected by the majority of people reading it. But this is how I see it.

Nowhere in Scripture do I find a promise from God for death with dignity. In fact, I see a Bible full of deaths in the most atrocious manner. People are eaten by wild animals, filleted open by swords, crushed by stoning, have their heads served on a platter, and are cut up into tiny pieces and distributed about the country. The legendary deaths of the apostles were no less gruesome, with beheadings and crucifixions and being torn apart by wild dogs. Death with dignity is an invention of man, not God.

We assign many characteristics to our God. He is omniscient, omnipotent, and omnipresent. He is intimately involved with those who are unfortunate enough to find themselves in a hospital fighting for their lives. He is certainly present.

And He is omniscient. He alone knows the time and the place of our death. When we take things into our hands and shut off the machines, we usurp that knowledge, determining when and how someone shall die.

And He is omnipotent. I have seen innumerable patients who have suffered cardiac arrest who were resuscitated. People who were dead are brought back to life. However, there are limitations. Although Jesus Himself and Lazarus arose from the dead, I have yet to see someone arise who had the sheet pulled over them and were carried to the morgue. When we terminate life support and shut off the machines, it is a permanent end to that person's life. Although I have no doubt that God could resurrect someone from the morgue, it doesn't happen with any regularity. What does happen is miraculous healing, and I have seen this often—a person with no chance for survival pulling through against all odds. So when we shut off the machines to give someone death with dignity, we *effectively* remove the opportunity for an omnipotent God to work a healing miracle in that person's life.

No one wants to *needlessly* prolong someone's life and suffering, such as when someone has a massive stroke, inoperable cancer, or a truly fatal illness. But when people are "stuck" on machines in a critical illness, there are two types of errors that can be made. We can play God by keeping someone alive that God is trying to call home. Or we can play God by terminating someone's life that God still plans to use. We can play God in either direction.

When someone has suffered severe brain injury, brain death occurs. This is actually fairly easy to determine.

There is a totally flat brainwave tracing. There is no response to any painful stimuli. There aren't even any reflexes—the pupils don't dilate, the patient doesn't gag when the back of the throat is stimulated, they don't blink when the cornea is touched. They don't even breathe on their own.

But sometimes there is not complete brain death. The patient is in a coma with some basic functioning. And sometimes it is impossible to tell if that patient will ever recover. I have seen people in a deep coma with no response for months suddenly awake and become fully normal. Generally speaking, however, if someone appears to have a severe brain injury and is in an *irreversible* coma, a "vegetable," then I don't know anyone who would consider it appropriate to keep them alive permanently on machines. The problem is that we as humans are unable to make that determination accurately in every case. For the Christian, I am not sure when the Holy Spirit departs the damaged mind.

I am human and fallible. I make mistakes. I cannot claim to know God's exact will for each and every patient. I make errors. And so do we all. And if we must make a mistake, which one shall it be? Needlessly prolonging life and suffering, or prematurely ending life? I completely discard the notion of "death with dignity" when faced with these decisions. I don't really care what your state of dignity is. I want to be obedient to God.

Here is what I do know. God is completely in control. He knows the appointed time of our deaths. And nothing we can do can stop it. If He is calling someone home, no power on earth, no medicine I can give, no treatment man has devised will stop it. You can put people on respirators, hook them up to dialysis, and feed them with tubes and pumps, but all of man's machines will not keep someone alive whom God has determined should pass away. He always overrides man's designs in these matters, and you cannot keep someone alive on machines forever. Yet we can end a life easily, and with the few exceptions God has shown in the Bible, that decision is permanent. I would rather err on the side of needlessly prolonging life, knowing that God will easily put an end to my foolish maneuverings, rather than prematurely ending a life. There is some security in knowing that while you can permanently end a life, you cannot permanently extend one.

Well, that means making people suffer. Not only do they suffer an "undignified" death, they may suffer for weeks in an intensive care unit or somewhere else. But God determines how long this will be. And if you are, say, sixty, you have lived around three thousand weeks. I don't think an extra two or three weeks, or even a month, of suffering is a huge price to pay if you can ultimately survive.

And what about "quality" of life? I don't see a biblical promise of a quality life either. People in the Bible suffered from many problems for many years, including leprosy and blindness. Even Paul had a thorn in his side that he prayed would be taken from him on three occasions. People say, "I wouldn't want to live that way." Well, a lot of people live with diseases and handicaps and deformities who wouldn't *want* to live that way. As modern man, we want quality control over our lives, no suffering, and death with dignity. I am not sure that any of that is promised by God. And God may desire that you live with a stroke and partial paralysis for the rest of your days to the end of life, even as He desires that a child born with Down's syndrome struggle from birth onward as life begins.

There is one final thought for the Christian. If you believe in eternal life with God that is given by having a saving relationship with His Son Christ, then death will transport you into the presence of God. Pain and suffering will be relieved, and you begin eternity with Him. When you look at forever and ever and ever, delaying that moment for some weeks or months does not seem excessive, even if that time is futile.

However, if you do not have that saving relationship with Christ, then death will begin an eternity of *real* suffering, forever and ever and ever. I wonder if we should hasten that in an effort to relieve temporary suffering here on earth.

Perhaps we should be quicker to let the Christian go to their eternal reward and fight even harder to hold on to the unsaved, hoping and praying that there will be an opportunity to change that destiny.

Service As Relief

> After that, He poured water into a basin and began to wash the disciples' feet, and to wipe them with the towel with which He was girded.
>
> John 13:5

The French philosopher Rene Descartes wanted to see if he could determine what was real. He did this by a process called "systematic doubt." He analyzed everything he could think of, asking, "Can I prove that this exists?" He came to the conclusion that nothing could be proven completely, that everything could, in fact, be an illusion. There was one exception—himself. The only thing that he knew for certain that existed was himself. Even if his body, his limbs, and his senses were an illusion, he knew that at some basic level, he existed. He knew this because he could think. In Latin, this is expressed as, "*Dubito, ergo cogito, ergo sum*," known in philosophical circles simply as, "The Cogito." Translated, it says, "I doubt, therefore I think, therefore I am."

Wherever you are, you are always there with yourself. You can't get away from yourself if you tried. That is one thing that is always for certain. You are always there. Your problems are always someplace too. They are either at work, at home, in your marriage, or even within your own body. And regardless of where they are, you can always find them; some you can run away from, and some you will always carry with you. Your thoughts can always be directed, if you wish, to you, your situation, and your problems. You don't have to worry about losing them.

Not feeling any pain is a bad thing, feeling pain can be useful, and too much pain can be harmful. The adequate treatment of pain is important, and inappropriate treatments for pain can be harmful. Suffering causes pain, and our efforts so far have been to prevent unnecessary suffering and minimizing what suffering occurs. We have tried to do this by direct efforts and not by simply changing our perception of suffering.

Suffering and pain are intertwined. Suffering is the condition you are in, and pain is what you experience from that condition, just as an illness is your condition, and physical and mental pain are what you experience from that illness. The appropriate relief of pain is a worthy goal. Sometimes, however, we try to medicate ourselves to relieve pain by drugs or alcohol. This often causes more problems, suffering, and pain.

One of the problems with pain is that it focuses our attention on the source of the pain. When you have pain, that is often all you can think of, and the pain and your condition occupies your thoughts almost exclusively. This is why the adequate and appropriate relief of pain is useful; it allows you to function while the condition heals or changes. Certainly stopping the source of the suffering is the best way to stop the pain; there is nothing like passing a kidney stone to stop that pain. But if the condition cannot be changed immediately, then while we are doing the things we need to help it resolve, waiting for it to resolve, or praying for it to resolve, we may benefit from reducing the pain that we experience. This may be true even if we have a condition that will never improve.

Service to others may help in this regard. This seems very paradoxical. How could helping others help you? It works in the sense that it removes your focus from yourself. It is hard to focus on your pain when you are focused on someone else's. Like a pain medication that prevents you from experiencing the pain of an operation, service to others can help keep you from experiencing some of the pain of your suffering.

There are several caveats here. Service comes more naturally for some people than for others. It is defined as a category of spiritual gifts, meaning that when the Holy Spirit comes into your life, you are given a gift for use in furthering God's kingdom. It is not given out to everyone in equal measure.

Secondly, we are often laden with a sense of shame when we compare our level of service with that of others. We are all expected to serve others to some degree, but some people have a greater gift in this area than others. You would not feel a sense of shame if you could not throw a baseball from center field all the way to home plate just because someone else could. You aren't expected to serve to the same degree as everyone else either. You are expected to do what you can with what you have.

Thirdly, there are many ways to serve. Helping out locally with the crisis pregnancy center is no less worthy than going on a mission trip to Cambodia, which is no less worthy than financially supporting the pregnancy center or mission trips. They are all ways of serving. However, in terms of reducing your experience of pain, the more you are physically present with those people with needs, the more effectively your focus will change. Your focus is less likely to change for very long just by writing a check. Getting your hands dirty building something is likely to work much better. And just like pain medication, this is likely to be temporary relief. When the pain medication wears off or the service stops, there you are again with your pain. You have to repeat the dose. But that is the whole point. You are always there, and so are your problems. You can always come back to them whenever you want. They are there waiting for you, and even in service to others, you cannot run away from them.

This is not simply a method of attitude adjustment, a way to change your perspective, like the old maxim about the man with no shoes feeling sorry for himself until he saw a man with no feet. There appears to be something therapeutic in serving others, especially when the suffering is accompanied by depression. I have seen many people who were worn down by their worries who have had their spirits lifted by serving others, even to the point of excitement. It feels good.

And like any pain relief, too much can be a bad thing—an overdose. It is possible to overdo service to others, to the neglect of your loved ones and yourself. Fatigue and exhaustion can set in, especially if standards are set too high. You must use good judgment to ensure that you will have strength to deal with your own problems when you return to them.

Helping Others Suffer

> Blessed be the God and Father of our Lord Jesus Christ, the Father of mercies and God of all comfort, who comforts us in all our tribulation, that we may be able to comfort those who are in any trouble, with the comfort with which we ourselves are comforted by God.
>
> 2 Corinthians 1:3-4

Every weekday I drive to work beginning around six in the morning. By seven fifteen or so, I have a scalpel in my hand, ready to inflict pain on someone. They will not immediately feel it, as they are asleep. But in a few hours, when they awake, they will begin to feel pain, which we will control with medicines. Each day the pain will get better, and they will go home to recuperate, hopefully to return to an active and healthy life. Once a week, I see recovering patients in the office, and it encourages me to keep inflicting pain on others. This is because of the results. They come back to the office free of angina or shortness of breath, able to walk distances for the first time in months or years. The suffering that occurs under my hands results in healing, and it is the price demanded and paid to eliminate the greater suffering that led that person to me.

And once in a while someone dies. In almost all cases, the operation was a success and the heart was fixed, but the lungs or kidneys fail, or a stroke occurs. And someone loses a spouse, a father, a sibling, or even a son or daughter. Sometimes the operation contributes to the end of a sixty-year marriage. And I played a role in that.

My job requires that I be used simultaneously as an instrument of healing and of suffering.

We are often called upon to assist in helping others to suffer. As their medic, you must know the ways to help them. As with medicine, the first rule is to "do no harm." For heaven's sake, do not read the parts of this book dealing with logic to them in their anguish. The first need of the sufferer is love, not logic. Especially when someone's suffering is severe and acute. There will be a time later to discuss the heavy philosophical stuff. Right now, they don't need your brain; they need your shoulder.

When I was a medical student, I was working with a cardiologist when we had to go in the middle of the night and take care of a young woman who was a heavy smoker. She'd had a severe heart attack and was in shock. We got her stabilized and went into the waiting room to talk to her family. This was in the 1980s, when smoking was still allowed in hospitals, and when we walked in, we could hardly see, much less breathe. There were probably twenty family members in there puffing away.

Gasping for breath, the cardiologist said, "Can we put those things away? We wouldn't be here right now in the middle of the night if it weren't for smoking!" And they all guiltily extinguished their cigarettes. However, generally speaking, this is the wrong time to make that kind of point. So the second thing is that when someone is acutely suffering, you should avoid lecturing. There are some people who are in severe denial, and they do need to be taken to school repeatedly to see the source of their self-inflicted misery. But the climax of the catastrophe may be the wrong time.

Thirdly, while you may not be advised to lecture someone at the wrong time, you may be advised not to rescue them either. God has ordained consequences for sins. We can learn from both lectures and experience. As someone once said, we develop good judgment from experience and we develop experience from bad judgment. Some people need all the help they can get in the midst of their suffering, including mercy and comfort. Some people need to feel the brunt of their misconduct. Although we are not all wise like our heavenly Father, as healers, we may need to make some kind of diagnosis for our patient. If they are being chastened for sin, you should not abandon them, but you should not interfere with God's plan for them either.

As we have said, all suffering is not the same. The main thrust of this book is that there are different types of suffering, and we are to try and determine which type we are experiencing so that we can apply the correct remedy. We should try and assist our friend who is suffering to do that. Our fourth goal, then, is to help them do that spiritual gut check and encourage them not to do it forever. If they have determined that there is no sin causing their suffering, then I would gently try and direct them to the point where they stop asking the wrong "why?"

You must realize that every person, like every patient, is different. Sometimes I will have a young, robust patient who is five days out from his heart surgery and who is still lying around in bed moaning and complaining with extended self-pity. I will explain to him that the eighty-three-year-old great-grandmother has already walked the halls twice that morning, hoping to motivate him to get off his rear end. And then I will have some little old lady who has really been near death, who is struggling to survive, and all I can do is stroke her head. Just as all suffering is not the same, all people are not, and you must try and determine as best as you can what will help them the most.

The rules of etiquette and common sense apply. Do not attempt to minimize their suffering, saying, "It's not that bad," or, "Look how much worse it could be." A change of perspective can sometimes be useful in managing suffering, but just as this has not been the goal of this book, neither should it be your goal. The camera will eventually pull back from the zoom position, and the bigger picture will eventually be seen. And likewise, do not trot out your own stories of your big ordeals. There will be a time and place to share what you have learned from your struggles, but showing someone your old gallbladder scar when they have a fresh chest incision is really gauche.

Finally, when I have a problem with one of my patients that I cannot solve, I refer them to a specialist. And you need to know when to do that too. You aren't expected to know how to manage or cure all forms of suffering. But you need to recognize when to call in serious help, such as pastoral counseling or even substance abuse professionals. Administering first aid on the roadside is always appropriate, but don't delay them getting to the hospital and the intensive care they need.

I have helped thousands of people suffer through illness, and I have at some point or another gotten all of the above points wrong. I can only give you advice and a list of things to do by making mistakes. Please learn from mine.

Suffering for You

> For when we were still without strength, in due time Christ died for the ungodly. For scarcely for a righteous man will one die; yet perhaps for a good man someone would even dare to die. But God demonstrates His own love toward us, in that while we were still sinners, Christ died for us.
>
> Romans 5:6-8

I am from Wilson, a small town in eastern North Carolina. In days gone by, that part of the state was the tobacco capital of the United States. About seventy miles to the east lies another small town, Plymouth, which is located on the Roanoke River. Its most recent population is about four thousand souls. It was there that Jack Lucas was born in 1928, son of a tobacco farmer.

Jack was quite an athlete in junior high school, and was stout and muscular. By the time he was fourteen years old, he stood about five feet, eight inches tall and weighed around 180 pounds. It was this impressive build that allowed him to fake his way into the Marines in 1942, claiming he was seventeen. He had a burning desire to see combat, and would allow nothing to stand in his way. By 1944, he had worked his way over to Honolulu, and it was there that his deception fell apart when he wrote a letter to his girlfriend and disclosed his age. Plans were made to ship him back to the States, but he stowed away on a ship headed to Iwo Jima. He turned seventeen while at sea.

He joined a four-man rifle team and headed into battle the day after landing on Iwo Jima. While in a ravine, the team came under fire, and two grenades were tossed into their midst. To save the lives of the others, Jack jumped on the first grenade and buried it under himself in the volcanic sand. He then reached out, grabbed the other grenade, and pulled it under him as well. His body absorbed the explosion and saved the lives of his fellow Americans.

Falling on a grenade to save others in combat is almost always fatal. It has been said that this specific act has resulted in more Medal of Honor citations than any other act of bravery. And lest you think that this type of heroism is only something seen long ago, you should know that all four of the Medal of Honor recipients in the Iraq War received them posthumously, and two of these were for falling on grenades.

Jesus tells us in John 15:13, "Greater love has no one than this, than to lay down one's life for his friends." The act of heroism of these men reminds us of Christ willingly sacrificing himself to save us. In the battle of God against Satan, Jesus knew of the lives that would be eternally saved by his death, but it somehow seems different. Those courageous soldiers died trying to save their comrades; Jesus died for God's enemies. "For if when we were enemies we were reconciled to God through the death of his Son, much more, having been reconciled, we shall be saved by his life" (Romans 5:10).

I, who sit here writing this, and you, who sit there reading this, are doing so because brave men before us died to make it safe for us to do so. Even now, as your eyes track these words, men and women are putting themselves into great peril for us, and yes, some of them are dying. Because of the clandestine nature of the work of some of them, you will never know of their sacrifice. They die violently, but quietly, and their passage will be unknown to you. Few but the grieved widows and fatherless children will know the cost of our freedom to live as we please here in America. Although Christ must receive our highest praise and honor, by his death giving us life everlasting, let us also give honor to those whose ultimate gift gives us liberty. This book has been about dealing with our sufferings, and I trust it has given you a survival manual for doing so, equipping you with the ability to determine the cause of your suffering, what you can do to prevent it or at least manage it, and how you can avoid the pitfalls that can come to the unwary as you endure your suffering. I know that your suffering, past or present, has been painful for you, and also that, for some, only passing on will end their suffering here on earth. The fact that you can hold this book in your hands, however, means that you have not yet suffered the ultimate sacrifice. Many have done so for you.

Jack Lucas was one of the few people to survive falling on a grenade. Only one of the grenades exploded, the other being a dud. Near death, he underwent twenty-six operations and still had more than two hundred pieces of shrapnel remaining in his body. He was the youngest recipient of the Medal of Honor since the Civil War. He passed away in June, 2008, at the age of eighty.

Many of us will go on living carrying reminders of our suffering, some with physical scars and others with shrapnel in their souls. With each challenge the Lord in His wisdom sends us, we know that he will work it to the good of those that love him and will ultimately bring glory to Him. I pray that whatever suffering is past you, is upon you, or is yet to come will be made more bearable by what has been contained in this little book. Jack Lucas did more than survive his injuries; he helped win a war. Ultimately, God promises us more than surviving the suffering. Through his Son Jesus Christ, he promises victory over all.

A Brief Summary

I would like to briefly summarize the necessary steps to eliminate or minimize suffering.

1. You must have a saving faith in Jesus Christ. This will remove you from the category of punishment, reserved for nonbelievers and having no redemptive qualities. This allows you access to God the Father and the Holy Spirit for guidance and unlocks the Scriptures for you to understand.

2. We should try to establish which category of suffering describes our situation. The most important thing we need to do is the spiritual gut check, whereby we determine if we are in or out of God's will. This is done by turning to God's Word, prayer, seeking guidance from other believers, and examining our life circumstances. God will not lie to us if we sincerely seek to determine if we are in His will or not. If we are not, then we are being chastened, and we need to repent and ask forgiveness.

3. We must not spend extraordinary lengths of time beating ourselves up doing the spiritual gut check. This in itself causes great suffering. We should try and ask the correct "why," meaning that we try to determine the cause of our suf-

fering, if at all possible. We may not be able to identify some higher purpose to our suffering. Sometimes sin happens, and it is not corrective or educational. It is not all about you.

4. If we are being pruned, we must not resist. We must not fight back against God.

5. If we are in spiritual warfare, we must fight back against Satan. We must utilize the armor God provides and above all enlist other believers. *Never fight your spiritual battles alone.*

6. If we are suffering to glorify God or for Christ, we can petition for relief or for the power to endure in a way that brings glory to God. If we are suffering to bring glory to God, we must pray for the miracle within us that will allow us to do that. If we are suffering for Christ, we pray for relief. This latter problem is an exceedingly rare occurrence for most of us.

7. We should avoid fruitless and counterproductive complications, such as making excuses, excessive self-pity, becoming angry with God, carrying inappropriate shame, becoming envious, engaging in denial, or allowing impatience to rule us.

8. Prayer is a vital part of the relief of our suffering.

9. We can look for miracles in the everyday solutions to our problems, as well as divine intervention.

10. Service to others can provide some relief for our suffering.

I close now with a look from the past to the present, never knowing the future.

Epilogue

> ...being confident of this very thing, that He who has begun a good work in you will complete it until the day of Jesus Christ.
>
> Philippians 1:6

At the beginning of this book, I described for you a childhood beset with health problems, often spent in the hospital or recuperating at home. I was often unable to do many of the usual childhood activities, although I was frequently well between bouts of illness. Still, I missed a great deal of school. While other kids were out learning the basics of baseball, I was in an oxygen tent. So I did the only thing you could really do when you were in the hospital that much. I read. And read. And read.

I read on everything. I read science, books on chemistry and physics and biology and astronomy. I read books on military history and aviation and detective stories and science fiction. I read Mark Twain and Isaac Asimov. I read Jules Verne, H. G. Wells, and Alfred Hitchcock. I read of the exploits of heroes of the past as well as of those of the current time, including surgeons such as Michael DeBakey and Denton Cooley. In the process, I became a complete *nerd*, although the term had not been invented yet.

I could build a radio from scrap parts and assemble

any type of airplane model. I could dissect a fish and explain all of its anatomy or demonstrate the parts of a paramecium under the microscope. I could describe to you all of the major "seas" on the moon or the components of the rocket ships that would get you there. But being nothing but a reader and an introvert, I had no social skills. I was never around other people enough to truly develop those skills or become comfortable with strangers.

This persists to this day. I do not use my childhood illness as an excuse. Like Paul, I too have a thorn in my side that I pray will be removed, and as God sanctifies me, I believe it will be taken from me, one micron at a time. Among many shortcomings, it stands out the most, and it is as noticeable as if my forehead were painted purple. It is an un-Christlike part of me, a lack of warmth and humanness to people I do not know.

As a child, I could not see beyond the past or the present. As an adult, I can look back at my past and my present, which was that child's future.

Suppose that child, who was reading in an oxygen tent at two o'clock in the morning, developed a lifelong habit? And although he did not learn to communicate very well with others directly, he was able to write? As a child of medicine, he came to practice medicine. And as he suffered as a child, now his job is to alleviate that suffering. What if that was God's plan all along?

And now the child who suffered but loved to read can write a book that will help relieve other people's suffering. I go to work every day and see people suffer. Not just my patients or their families but the people I work with every day. They have heartaches and illnesses and lose loved ones. There is no surgery I can perform on them to make them better.

When you are suffering, there may be no obvious reason. And endlessly seeking the reason may lead to only more suffering. Like Job, it may never be revealed to us. And the pointlessness, as we perceive it, makes it more difficult to endure. We can only know the present and the past, not the future. We cannot know how our present suffering, meaningless as it seems, may be used for God's purposes later on.

For me, it has been forty years between my childhood sufferings and writing this book; it is conceivable that what I have written will alleviate as much suffering as the scalpel that I will pick up tomorrow morning. With God's blessing, I pray that it will be so.

Notes

1. Henry Blackaby, Richard Blackaby, and Claude King, *Experiencing God*, (Nashville: LifeWay Press, 2007).

2. Henry Blackaby, and Richard Blackaby, *Hearing God's Voice*, (Nashville: Broadman and Holman, 2002).

3. Glines, Carol, *Four Came Home,* (Missoula: Pictoral Histories Publishing Company, 1996).

4. George Mueller, *Answers to Prayer*, (Chicago: Moody Publishers, 1984), 6.